JESUS OF NAZARETH,
A PERSON LIKE US?

JESUS OF NAZARETH,
A PERSON LIKE US?

ROGER LENAERS, S.J.

CARYSFORT PRESS

A Carysfort Press Book in association with Peter Lang
Jesus of Nazareth: A Person Like Us?
by Roger Lenaers, S.J.

A translation by Dan Farrelly of *Jesus von Nazareth, ein Mensch wie wir?*
published by Edition Anderswo, Kleve 2015

First published in Ireland in 2016 as a paperback original by
Carysfort Press, 58 Woodfield, Scholarstown Road
Dublin 16, Ireland

ISBN 978-1-78997-040-1

Typeset by Carysfort Press
Cover design by eprint limited

CONTENTS

CHAPTER ONE

There was a time when Jesus of Nazareth was only thought about and written about uncritically, in keeping with church piety. Then came the Enlightenment and with it Hermann Samuel Reimarus (1694-1768). He was an absolute innovator, the first for more than fifteen centuries who dared to undertake an historical-critical investigation of the content of the Gospels and, in so doing, to follow reason. His thoughts have proved to be for the most part fundamentally correct. In the 250 years since his work was published, much that was contained in his then new ideas has been accepted. But the concrete conclusions he drew from his interpretation of the Gospels were often wrong: for example, that he interpreted the Resurrection of Jesus as a scheme which his disciples organized so as to profit, as long as possible after his death, from the veneration the people had for Jesus. He knew that his interpretations of the life of Jesus would arouse vigorous criticism and antagonism. For this reason he did not publish the results of his studies himself, but gave them to some friends to read. Only after the death of Reimarus in 1768 did Lessing, one of the great thinkers of the German Enlightenment, decide to publish part of it, although in a tame form as "Fragments" from the work of an anonymous author.

The appearance of these so-called "Wolfenbüttel Fragments" 1774-1778 led, as was expected, to a flood of polemical writings and aggressive reactions, attacks on the person of the meanwhile deceased author, attempts, at all costs, to defend the supernatural in the Gospels, and rebuttals of these attempts. Clearly, Reimarus had touched a very sensitive nerve.

Anyone who wants to form an idea of the ensuing battles regarding the historical Jesus, with the resulting multiplicity of contradictory Jesus images, only needs to read the *Geschichte der Leben-Jesu-Forschung which* Albert Schweitzer published in 1906. His superb historical study leads inevitably to the conclusion that it is not possible to discover the genuine historical Jesus. The source material one would need to draw on is much too unreliable. First, each of Jesus's disciples who spoke about him after his death had his own somewhat differently coloured memory of Him, and these differences were multiplied according to the psychology of the listeners who passed on the message they received. And, as well, the circumstances in which they lived had no small influence on the view they formed. Then the Aramaic traditions in their different forms were translated into Greek and recounted further. But obviously every translation is an interpretation and an adaptation. Finally, 40 years after the death of Jesus someone (today it is generally accepted that it was Mark), wrote – with the help of this diverse and sometimes contradictory material – a whole story which was to outline the activity of Jesus, together with his message. But this story was again the product of Mark's own notions. Then Matthew and Luke built further on this foundation. On the basis of these many lenses between the historical reality and the written result – the Gospels – the white light of historical reality only comes to us refracted into many colours. What that white light really was like thus remains hidden. We see Jesus only through the many eyes of the devout community, and these many eyes did not at all see the same thing.

The Figure of Jesus in the Modern Historical-Critical Jesus Literature

Most of these historical-critical studies from the 19th and 20th centuries led to results in which very little was left of the picture of Jesus as it had been shaped by Western culture. Yet again scientific truth, now in the shape of historical reliability, seemed fundamentally to contradict traditional beliefs. In the 19th century there were even authors who maintained that the historical existence of that figure of Jesus which was always evading the historian's grasp was a fairy tale or a myth. These authors also intended hereby to deny the Church all credibility, since it was seen as putting the brakes on modernity. Without an historical Jesus there would be no Church which could call on his authority.

One might have thought that interest in the person of Jesus of Nazareth would, in the meantime, have waned, for the critical ideas of unbelieving modernity penetrate the whole of society. Churches are emptying visibly, and Christian writings are certainly not bestsellers. However, new books about Jesus are continually appearing – a clear proof that despite everything there is still much interest in the person of Jesus, for a publisher will not promote any book for which he does not believe there will be sufficient sales at least to cover his costs.

Naturally the intention and focus vary with different authors. There are still those who, despite Albert Schweitzer, try to uncover the historical figure of Jesus: for example, with the help of historical analysis of the stormy period, full of uprisings, in which he lived. These authors were convinced that this age would have left its mark on Jesus so that in this way he becomes tangible. That led to the image of a failed socio-political Messias pretender. This is, for example, the way the American Muslim, Reza Aslan, sees him in his successful book *The Zealot*, to which we will return. Others try to work out, by means of very exact text analysis, what were the original words of Jesus himself and what – amongst the rest of the words ascribed to him – could have been the contribution of tradition. This is the focus of the authors who belong to the American *Jesus Seminar*. In this they have to move a long way from the field of the canonical Gospels, scour the apocryphal gospels, and also track down the Jesus-words handed down by the Fathers of the Church. Others examine the Jesus images which have come and gone since the Enlightenment and sometimes astound us: as, for example, the image of a Jesus who, during a childhood that is unknown to us, would have become a pupil of wise men in India or in Egypt, or who, after his only apparent death on the cross and recovery, withdrew to the Orient. Again others, like Josef Ratzinger, attempt, with consummate scholarship and profound spirituality, to make traditional dogmatic ideas acceptable.

Most of those modern authors are no longer what the Church deems to be believers; some are explicitly non-believers; but all are fascinated by that puzzling figure which emerges from the Gospels and, for us Christians, constitutes the kernel of our faith. We also call ourselves after him, at least by the second name Christ which we gave him ourselves and which obviously was not his family name. Christus is a Greek name of distinction, a glorifying name, which says what his followers saw in him and still see. It is the passive past participle of the Greek word that means "anointing". This term "Anointed One" was used in ancient Israel most especially for the king. There kings were not crowned, but anointed. The anointing of young David to kingship by the prophet Samuel, as it is narrated in 1 Samuel 16 with great literary skill, is evidence of this.

When the kingdom of David was dissolved after the death of his son Solomon and was later taken over first by the Assyrians, then by the Babylonians, then by the Persians, then by Alexander the Great and his Macedonians, then finally by the Romans, the "Anointed One" became a mythical figure which the Jews yearned for as their salvation (and which the orthodox amongst them still watch for). The certainty that he would come was guaranteed by Yahweh, they thought, for the Bible proclaimed it and was, after all, God's own word. And at his coming, they believed he would with the help of Yahweh make Israel free again and powerful and prosperous. The word "Messiah" comes from the Hebrew form of that mythical title for a king, *maschiach*. In the view of Jesus's disciples, he was that long-awaited Messiah. Only his wretched death would open their eyes to a different, deeper, no longer socio-political meaning of this title.

It is obvious that the Jesus of most modern Jesus books is far removed from the notions we encounter in Church pronouncements and in devout literature. There we have the impression that he belongs to a mythical world in which the laws governing the reality we experience no longer play a role. He is supposed to come from a divine world down into ours and to have been born of a virgin. He could walk on water, feed more than five thousand people with five loaves of bread and two fishes, change six hundred litres of water into six hundred litres of wine, calm a raging storm with a single word, bring someone back to life in whom decomposition had already set in, and much more. He was even able, a few days after his own bloody and violent death, to rise up by exercising his own powers, healthy and immortal, from his grave.

That is the Church's traditional view of Jesus, which is much more that of a mythical being than that of an historical person. For modern critics the Jesus presented traditionally by the Church is a product of the imagination, a pious fiction masking a Jewish figure from the first century AD which we are not in a position to reconstruct. Whoever accepts these impossible things which are related about him is living in a pre-scientific past and is incurably blind to reality.

We know too little about him with certainty

The sparse historical sources of non-Christian origin, like some sentences found in the writings of the Hellenised Jew Flavius Josephus or Tacitus or Suetonius, tell us very little about him: only that he was a Palestinian Jew who, during the reign of Emperor Tiberius, gathered followers around him in Galilee, and in the 30s was crucified by the Prefect of Judaea, Pontius Pilate, for rebellion against the Roman Empire. It is curious that the dating of events of world history is still based on the birth year of this historically insignificant man from Nazareth.

If we want to hear more about his life we have to turn to the Gospels. These are the four little books written about him by unknown followers between the years 70 and 100 after his death. These books are somewhat biographical, but without thereby being biographies. In any case, these are the most detailed witnesses that have come down to us. But between the image of Jesus seen there and the historical Jesus there are some decades of oral tradition stemming from his followers and admirers – the faithful – with the tendency which is common in hagiography to glorify the revered master, even at the expense of truth. Quite clearly, historical circumstances have also influenced the written accounts based on oral tradition. An obvious example is the destruction of Jerusalem – for the Jews an indelible memory – which occurred 40 years after the death of Jesus and which was then woven into his words. Then there are the persecutions to which his followers were later exposed and which he is supposed to have foretold in detail while he was still a successful itinerant preacher and healer.

All of this casts doubt on the historical reliability of the image of Jesus as it appears in the Gospels. Again and again one asks oneself whether this or that statement by Jesus really originates from him or whether it has not really been put into his mouth by the evangelist; and whether this or that amazing deed attributed to him corresponded to the reality or was not rather the fruit of imaginative mythical veneration by the community of believers at the time – a half century after his death.

What, then, is the intention of this present book? It does not at all aim at discovering the historical Jesus. As I have indicated, that is a sheer waste of time. The primary aim is to free the believer's message about Jesus from the mythology spun around him from time immemorial, closing off modern man's access to the inspiring figure of Jesus. Likewise, the book aims to free this figure of its clearly unhistorical patina. In earlier times this unhistorical aspect was not noticed, or, if it was, it was accepted uncritically on the erroneous assumption that everything written in the Gospels is the word of God and therefore, despite all historical improbability – or even impossibility – had to be affirmed. Moreover, there was the conviction that our salvation did not depend on historical truth but only on confessing the true faith as taught by Church authority.

One might hope that in the meantime Church authorities would, at least to some extent, have adopted the modern scientific and therefore anti-mythological approach. But apparently that is the case only to a very modest extent. Church leadership has no problem with believing in a mythical Jesus, a God in human form. And for the faithful it is still far less a problem. Their lack of awareness is to be accounted for by the fact that the leadership, consciously or unconsciously, confirms and reinforces that mythological image of Jesus. Every Sunday the faithful are summoned to church to hear texts which confirm them in their pre-modern conviction. The Gospel stories are particularly well suited to this, for they originate from a culture which is full of mythological notions. Also the sermon which follows the reading of the Gospel seldom or never reveals the reality which lies hidden in mythical garb. At best – and this is something of value in itself – the priest will leave the mythology be, and he will try to derive from the objectively unacceptable narrative some subjective spiritual meaning which was not what the evangelist had in mind. Although the priest lives in a modern scientific environment, through his belonging to a mythologically thinking Church he has himself grown up in an intellectually mythical climate, and his theological education has, for the most part, not helped him to escape from it. And who, during his studies, would have helped him to think about Jesus in a modern way? A theology professor who until a couple of decades ago openly ventured to do that would no longer have been sure of retaining his post. The Roman authority which feels called on to watch over purity of faith intervened in those days (and sometimes does even today), without pardon – with sackings, bans on speaking or writing, and other punishments – with a view to preventing the theologian from any longer spreading his ideas which were deemed to be against the faith.

What must this Church leadership think today when it sees the success of those modern Jesus biographies and views about Jesus? In those days such authors were excommunicated. For example, exactly 150 years ago Ernest Renan published his *Vie de Jésus*. The very first sentence of his book: "Jesus was born in Nazareth" was seen as scandalous, because with these words Renan was already denying the notion, unchallenged up to this point, that Jesus was born in Bethlehem – according to the two Gospel narrations about his childhood. The book landed promptly on the Index of forbidden books, which, rather than inhibiting its distribution, on the contrary promoted it.

In the meantime the Church leadership has had to become more cautious. It knows only too well how little is achieved by excommunication, and it hopes that members of the Church will not like the taste of this modern soup or at least will not want it as hot as it is dished up. It furthermore trusts in the powerful effect of the mythological counter-force with which the faithful are confronted every Sunday at Mass. It thinks that constant dripping hollows the stone. Unfortunately, it also works the other way round: the earlier mythological certainties are gradually being hollowed out by daily contradiction in the modern media. And this in a much more efficient way.

Because of this the believer has, in his search, the ever stronger creeping feeling that, in his confession of faith in Jesus, he is a rarity in modern society. And that is not what he wants to be. He wants to be a believer, but equally a person of today's world. Unfortunately, the mythological dressing up of the message of faith lies as a barrier in the path of this connection.

In freeing Jesus of his ancient mythological garb the modern Jesus biographers, despite all their deficiencies, achieve at least this much that is praiseworthy: that also modern people who are not to be fobbed off with pious mythology can still look up to Jesus with admiration. Reza Aslan, mentioned above, can serve as an example of this. The two decades of his critical preoccupation with the Gospels "have made of me", he writes, "a more honestly dedicated disciple of Jesus of Nazareth than I have ever been of Jesus Christ."

But with this departure from the mythological Jesus we have only travelled half of our journey. The mythology gradually woven about the person of Jesus was only the contemporary, and therefore pre-modern translation of that depth and fullness which the faithful of the time experienced in Jesus. We have to give quite different expression to this depth and fullness in this modern period which thinks and speaks in a radically different manner. The critical Jesus biographies have, as a rule, no eye for this depth and fullness precisely because their almost exclusive aim is to divest the historical Jesus of his mythical garb. But without that depth and fullness, which we certainly have to express otherwise than in earlier times, the critical view of Jesus is only the black and white image of a resplendent polychrome reality.

Precisely today it is absolutely necessary to free Jesus from the mythological cocoon into which the Church of the past has lovingly spun Him. But why today, precisely? Because until modernity became established, such a liberation was not at all necessary. The whole of pre-modern thinking was shot through with mythological notions and Jesus could only win when in this kind of thinking a vital place was assigned to Him. Until a few decades ago the image of Jesus formed by most of the readers of this book, and my own image of Jesus as well, was fundamentally still mythological. But in the world of modern culture, the Church's message about Jesus and his liberating and renewing role for humanity no longer finds, if pre-modern formulated, any resonance. It has simply become incomprehensible. The main reason is that the modern world has parted company with that whole world of mythological thinking.

The next chapter aims at explaining this in more detail. It will show that religion is essentially of a mythological nature and show why modernity had to take leave of that mythology. Anyone who has become sufficiently acquainted with the author's ideas through reading *The Dream of King Nebuchadnezzar* will not find much that is new in the next chapter – at most, a hopefully clear summary of the fundamental ideas of the author. Anyone who has no further need of this could omit reading the chapter.

CHAPTER TWO

From Pre-Modern to Modern, or from Religion to Atheism

Whether it is a matter of regret or not, the great majority of those baptized in Western society now care very little about Church membership. Without knowing or wishing it, by baptism they have been made members of the organization "Church" and for some years have, influenced by the cultural tradition of their parents, played along with the Church game –even quite happily: until they ate from the tree of knowledge and their eyes were opened and they saw that, like their Church, they stand there naked, and have no notion of what to do.

In Germany and in Austria it is possible to have one's decision to part company with the Church officially recognized. It is necessary to apply to the regional authorities, officially report one's wish to leave the Church, and sign a declaration to that effect. The real outcome is freedom from financial burdens which one had to take on as a declared member of the association that is the Catholic Church. In general, this step changes nothing at all in people's daily lives, which shows that belonging to the Church has had no influence on their behaviour. But if, in a chemical process, it is possible to take away a component without anything changing in the process and in the result, the total uselessness of that component is proven. Then faith is the salt that does not salt and, according to the words of the Gospel, can simply be thrown away. And it is, in fact, being thrown away. In large quantities. In Germany, every year a quarter of a million so-called faithful, in Austria about 50,000. These figures reveal, unfortunately, what in reality is hidden behind the façade of what is usually called faith: only hot air.

The financial advantage is, of course, particularly attractive when membership of the Church organization leaves a person completely cold. Is anyone who has not the slightest interest in football and consequently never looks at a game, likely to remain a paying member of a football club? Besides, in reality (and only what is real is important) has anyone who officially leaves the Church not already long since left it inwardly? And he has unofficially made it clear to those around him simply by systematically staying away from Church gatherings. What he has done is something similar to separation prior to divorce. But that does not exclude occasionally entering a church and honouring one or other of the traditional rituals, the meaning of which he or she no longer understands (and for the most part never did understand), as, for example, the baptism of a child in the family or a First Communion.

For many a faithful churchgoer it is a worrying puzzle that a rapidly growing majority in today's Western society is tired of dealing with the Church. The Church is, after all, the obvious guarantee of our well-being here on earth and after death, isn't it? Then why give up this guarantee? Surely this can only be a loss. And why are so many suddenly doing it now? And above all, why are the large majority of young people doing it, so that we are right to fear that, for want of members, nothing will be left of the Church around the year 2100?

What a modern believer, closely involved with the Church, wrote to me recently is symptomatic of what is happening in many families today: of his four children, all academics, three have become atheists, the fourth did have a Church marriage and can be reckoned among critical fringe Christians.

The "pious" people's answer to the scandal of this puzzle is, as a rule, hardly convincing. Some blame it on today's prosperity. Back in the time when there was hardship and war, people poured into the churches, didn't they? And so, in their eyes, a climate of threat and misery would be the ideal, as, for example in North Korea, and that ought to be our earnest desire. But here we are forgetting that it was not prosperity that, in the 19th century, drove the proletariat out of the Church and into the arms of anti-Church socialism (as communism was originally called) while the well-to-do class, in general, remained loyal to the Church. Others point the finger of blame at the lax indulgent attitude of modern parents who, in contrast to the good old days, immediately capitulate when their children resist going to church. But they don't ask where this unwillingness on the part of the children might come from. Or they blame the enticements of modern life. But why does the so highly praised and once so keenly practised church piety have so little appeal for the younger generation? Apart from some events like the World Youth Days, what the Church has to offer leaves them completely cold. If we want to find the real cause of the quick decline of the Church and, more generally, of religion in the modern Western world, we need to go a long way back in human history and get a bird's eye view of the historical phenomenon of religion. Christianity – one can also say the Church or the faith, from which one departs either by leaving the Church or no longer going to church – is only the Western form of that general human phenomenon that is religion. When someone leaves our form of religion, i.e. leaves the Church, this is done, as a rule, not in order to join another church or religion. One does hear from time to time of conversions to Islam, but even if there were a few thousand such cases per year, it is a small and dwindling number by comparison with the many tens of thousands who, every year, soundlessly or under protest leave the Church.

The Origin of the Phenomenon Religion

We don't know when this phenomenon came into being. Our far, far-off relatives, the primates, clearly do not know about it and probably never knew it. Yet they do have a modicum of intelligence and even an embryonic ethic, as modern studies of chimpanzees and bonobos have shown. These primates have empathy, look after members of their species when they are in difficulty, and acknowledge authority. However, for the emergence of religion we have to wait for the appearance of the species homo. Some time after the long process of this so-called hominization, which probably took some hundreds of thousands of years, primitive forms of what was to develop into religion appeared. Religion did not appear on earth ready-made the way the goddess Athena emerged from the head of Zeus. With the development of religion also evolution did not make any leaps.

Those primitive forms would have had mainly to do with those frightening natural phenomena which, for our ancient ancestors were inexplicable and in the face of which they felt completely defenceless, such as tornados, bushfires, thunder and lightning, the power of the waves, volcanoes, and earthquakes, and a sudden death. In their anxious need for an explanation and for protection they imagined that behind these phenomena of nature forces were hidden which were in every way completely superior to them. Subconsciously they conceived these powers as humanlike beings. And just as they preferred to forestall the anger of social authority figures – fathers, tribal chiefs or medicine men – and tried to placate them, they did not want to fall out with these supernatural powers. This is the source of the idea: "Fear produced the gods", which found great resonance in the Enlightenment period.

Although much of this is true, there is, however, also much that can be said against it, and even much of crucial importance. First, our ancestors also regularly encountered enjoyable natural phenomena, like spring or fertility or birth or the winter solstice, which were equally inexplicable, equally beyond the disposition of man, but not at all frightening. Thus the powers above were by no means all threatening. And just as there were means to secure the favour of those who exercised earthly power, it was thought that the same could be achieved by similar means with regard to the supernatural forces. Part of this was showing them proper respect and acknowledging their power and importance – that is where religious cult originates –, offering them presents – that is where we find cultic sacrifice –, listening to their earthly representatives, i.e. to people who gave the impression or maintained that they had a closer relationship to these powers than that which ordinary mortals enjoyed. And just as it is occasionally possible, with humble and insistent petitions, to get something from human beings, it was also thought possible to achieve this with the gods. Hence the prayers for good weather, a happy childbirth, a successful hunt, even for remission of punishment when one is afraid one might have offended the powers above. If what one prayed for, actually happened, one should not neglect giving thanks to the powers concerned. This list contains what is essential to the exercise of religion: humble acknowledgement of a power or powers above (or below, for there were also deities in the underworld), prayers of praise and thanksgiving, sacrifices, prayers of petition, obedience to the prescriptions of those people whom one believed to be speaking for the gods.

For those who entertain the fear hypothesis, this explanation of the origin of religion and its forms is grist to the mill. But whence did our ancestors have this tendency or need to see behind natural phenomena the operation of "gods" – all-powerful supernatural beings similar in form to human beings? Why did they not simply acknowledge their own helplessness and vulnerability and try, with all that lay in their power, to protect themselves from the threatening effects of natural phenomena, just as the primates are still doing? How is it to be explained that they believed in the existence of invisible powers resembling human beings, developed a whole cult system with regulations and punishments and made all expressions of their culture dependent on it? And that was done not just by some tribe or other. The phenomenon religion is found in all cultures, no matter how primitive or how highly developed – and indeed throughout the whole of human history.

Could it not be, then, that man has an innate, extremely vague sense, a kind of slumbering consciousness that, with all that exists, he belongs to a reality which encompasses and transcends both him and the whole cosmos? The confrontation with nature experiences which also transcends him, would then, again and again, awaken this slumbering inkling of an absolute transcendence which would appear related to the horizon of his consciousness. Not as transcendence in its pure form, but as inseparably connected with the phenomenon that awakens it. The transcendence experience would thereby each time assume the form of that concrete natural phenomenon, so that, for example, thunder and lightning would become the gods of thunder and lightning, acquiring a shape and a name, as, for example, Zeus or Thor. What appeared in human consciousness in all these forms was, in fact, the fundamental transcendent reality, in an impure, distorted, often barely discernible form, but nonetheless genuine. The polytheism born out of this (from the Greek *poly-*: "much" and *theos:* "divinity") was a first big step in surpassing the level on which primates still live. For a few hundred thousand years there was no essential change with regard to religion. But about 3,000 years ago there followed a second important step when, in the then culturally insignificant Judaism the multiplicity of supernatural powers finally had to yield, after long resistance, to a single (in Greek: *monos*) God, whom the Jews called Yahweh. This monotheism was characterized by an extraordinary dynamism. In less than two thousand years it spread over the whole world in two forms, as Christianity and as Islam, and to a large extent ousted the polytheism which, until then, had been dominant everywhere.

But today something unthinkable is happening, which can be considered a third step: the monotheism which was so dynamic is now, in its turn, being ousted in its own European heartland by a new ideology which had never existed in human history: atheism. The name with the negative Greek prefix a- indicates what is involved: the denial of what has been fundamental to all religions since the beginning of humanity: the existence of gods or of one almighty god outside the cosmos, upon whom the cosmos is in every respect totally and absolutely dependent, and who is in total control of all that we do. How did Western society – and only this society, for atheism is a purely Western phenomenon – arrive at the point of denying a certainty which has existed unchallenged and inviolate since the beginning of human history and even today is taken for granted by the greater majority of people?

This denial, is to be seen as caused in the first instance by the development of modern science. It is these sciences that have made it impossible for thinking people in the West to believe any longer in the reality of an almighty Theos existing in the highest and thus have produced atheism in the Western world. This atheism arose in a Europe which, for more than a thousand years, had adhered to Christian monotheism. It arose, indeed, in the 18th century in France which at that time was the dominant force in European thinking and culture. The birth of atheism did not resemble the sudden appearance of a meteor. It was the conclusion of a long process of growth which had begun in the 15th century with the rediscovery of Greek and Roman antiquity. For our theme, important above all is the rediscovery of its scientific heritage. The following century already saw the first powerful impulses of modern science which sprang from this ancient root. In the 17th century under the influence of geniuses like Galileo, Pascal, Descartes, and Newton this development accelerated its pace still further. This led, in the 18th century, to such new insights that people whose thinking had been formed by the medieval worldview completely lost their sense of security. The world no longer corresponded to the view they had inherited from the Middle Ages. It is not a vale of tears through which one, in suffering and prayer, ascended God's mountain; it is not the disappointing underside of a different, perfect world which determines everything here, controls what we do, rewards and punishes. It is rather a closed system which follows its own (in Greek *autos*) unchangeable laws (in Greek *nomos*); in other words, it is autonomous, immune to inroads from outside the cosmos. And these internal and immutable laws completely explain things which, for the lack of any explanation, had till then been ascribed to the influence of divine powers outside the cosmos.

Of all the natural phenomena in which earlier people thought they were seeing the forces from outside the cosmos at work, thunder and lightning were the most convincing and the most frightening. But in 1750, with the help of life-threatening experiments, Benjamin Franklin proved that lightning was only an electrical discharge – gigantic, but nevertheless purely natural – which had nothing to do with the intervention of God up above. In a thunderstorm one could further forget about Holy Water, palm leaves, and prayers. What was needed was a good lightning conductor on the roof.

After this first step of eliminating magic from nature, further steps kept on following, new discoveries of the natural character of many phenomena which had previously been ascribed to the intervention of a supernatural world. The spheres of divine intervention were steadily narrowed until in the end there was nothing left of them. Even clairvoyance, stigmata, apparitions and surprising healings, which used to count, without challenge, as revelations of a supernatural world, could now be explained definitively without recourse to a God above: intramundane forces sufficed.

Those interested in science in the early days had seen God continually at work in all things (cf. for example, the pious utterances of Isaac Newton in his *Principia mathematica*). But now they only saw the laws of nature at work everywhere, and everything which was seen earlier as proof of the reality of a supernatural world had now lost all validity. The God who had once been seen as extremely effective became an ineffectual God and it would not be long until from ineffectual He became irrelevant. At first the new thinking did not deny His existence. Ten thousand years of collective conviction cannot in a couple of decades – nor even in a couple of centuries – be extinguished by reason. People continued to believe that God did (probably) exist, but he did no longer play any role. Everything went on, with no problems, without him. So why then be preoccupied with him? The earlier, easily understandable eagerness to be on a good footing with him disappeared, together with the fear of being punished by him in an afterlife which is beyond our grasp. This brought with it that the Sunday church visits disappeared as well as the readiness to do or leave undone what a Church authority calling on God's will prescribed or forbade. Modernity, i.e. the new Western culture, was visibly becoming irreligious, atheistic.

However, it did not stop with our being able to look after ourselves and not needing recourse to God. It became ever clearer that, if God existed and if He wanted to intervene, He was not able to. In the chain of cause and effect there was no longer any space left for His intervention. Besides, such an intervention would damage the wonderful totality of the cosmos. In earlier times such miraculous interventions presented no problem, for people believed that everything was possible for God. Accordingly, He could even let the sun stand still for 24 hours in the zenith, as we read in the book of Joshue. That is, of course, sheer nonsense. All the laws of physics and astronomy would cease to be valid and the cosmos itself would cease to exist. Even a possibly existing God had to keep to the laws which rule nature. He could not abrogate them even for a moment without everything falling back into primeval chaos. Praying for His intervention, for rescue, success, victory, fine weather, a job – all of this became meaningless. What was taken for granted for a hundred thousand years suddenly no longer made sense. That other invisible world which, as was thought, influenced everything here and with which religion so keenly busied itself, no longer existed. What the Church said about it – and it had inordinately much to say without the slightest proof – was mythology.

Myths and Mythology

Of course, it was not mythology in the original sense of the word, which refers to the stories from a distant past about gods and beings similar to gods, who are invisible, immortal, powerful, all-knowing, and living in Olympus or in Walhalla. From the beginning, the Church had rejected this form of mythology as a product of the imagination and as incompatible with the truth of its own teaching. But in the eyes of modernity, the Church's own notions about another world are seen as mythology, albeit more spiritual and more reflected than the rather crude and anthropomorphic mythology of antiquity. For modernity, every view that contradicts the inner laws of the cosmos is mythological. This malady is to a high degree inherent in the Church's basic idea of a Theos, a God outside the cosmos, who can, whenever He likes, intervene in the cosmos and simply disable its laws, and thus is also found in all the stories and doctrines which emanate from this way of thinking.

Of itself, the Greek word *mythos* only means story, but in the broader sense it means a story which does not care about the impossibility or gross improbability of its content. Here, everything is played out on a level of reality where the laws of possible experience and of normality are no longer binding. Often, these old myths are stories with a double layer, a hidden meaning. They are images of human reality. Atheistic modernity reads and interprets them as such and approaches them mostly with respect and sympathy. But this is no longer the case when it comes to the Christian myths. The historically understandable aggressiveness of modernity towards the Church blinds it in this regard. The Christian myths are seen as mere fables, fairy tales, gossip, not to be taken seriously, unreal. Modernity really should not react in this way. Also with regard to these myths it should ask what deeper meaning they have, what message they contain. Unfortunately, that does not happen.

The reason for this is partly that the Church authorities do not present their own myths as myths, namely as images standing for something else, in the way they do in the case of pre-Christian myths. Instead, the Church maintains that its mythical texts describe actual reality, even though there is no concrete evidence available. And when they deduce from these myths demands and prohibitions to be imposed on society, the atheists have had enough. It is not possible, by appealing to an imaginary power outside the cosmos, to make demands in the real world of our cosmos that contradict its accepted insights and rules! The Church protests, just as decisively as atheism, when with regard to circumcision, honour killing, forced conversion, discrimination against women, etc. all of this is explained as the will of Allah. But it does not seem to be aware that its own demands and prohibitions regarding homophilia, compulsory celibacy, euthanasia, birth control, divorce, remarriage, exclusion of women from leadership roles in the Church, are equally open to criticism, because they are anchored in a supernatural world which has become unthinkable.

The Church on the Defensive

For the Church authorities, alarm bells started ringing from the very beginning of modernity, i.e. as early as the Enlightenment period. If there is no such thing as an invisible supernatural world which determines everything and on which the religions are based, the Church loses its *raison d'être*. From the very beginning, it was mainly devoted to the zealous worship of the God of the Old and New Testaments, whereby the good of humanity was entirely dependent on this worship. But with modernity none of this was left. On top of this the Church, and especially its leadership, was afraid that it would lose the influence and the wealth it had accumulated in the course of the centuries. Against this dangerous modernity, the Church went on the counter-offensive with all its strength, which had, in the meantime, been severely reduced. In the 19th century, one condemnation followed another. Even the many valuable things which it would later take on and bless, like freedom of conscience, the theory of evolution, democracy as a form of government, or the absoluteness of human rights – all of these the Church castigated in the severest terms.

This blind antagonism towards modernity caused the Church to become public enemy number one for those Europeans who were modern thinking. And since the Church defended the social status quo, which was an advantageous status for her, although for the masses it was mostly a status of repression and exploitation, she lost the earlier loyal support of the repressed and exploited. Later than the thinking class, the proletariat also became open to the new ideas of freedom and equality preached by socialism (socialism was, in the beginning, the name for what was later to be called "communism"). And the thinking behind this socialism was definitely anti-religious.

Let us be honest: even amongst the steadily shrinking minority of those in the West who stay with traditional teaching, many are not worried about what they profess. They profess things only because their sociological group does so and only where and when it does so, i.e. when it meets for the Sunday Mass in the church. Outside of the church building their beliefs hardly play a role, at any rate not one which would have an inspiring effect on their behaviour. Thus, when they give up their profession of faith and the practice of going to church, nothing changes in their lives: they remain just as egotistical or socially engaged, just as greedy or prepared to share as before. What used to keep them on the path of religion was not insight into the irreplaceable value of religion but often only the pressure of their environment. When this is gone because modern society as a whole is tending to move away from faith, very little is left of the earlier profession of the faith of these churchgoers. Although they might not see exactly why modernity has difficulties with traditional faith, they do sense that there are two masters at loggerheads with one another – and that they cannot serve both. The most basic reason for this incompatibility is the fact that all religions, including the Christian religion, have built their faith in an invisible, supernatural world on the then inexplicable nature of cosmic phenomena. But modern science has done away with this and has thereby destroyed the mythological foundations of the religions.

The increasingly speedy departure from the Christian faith in the West during the last decades is thereby first and foremost a departure from religion as a mythological residue of our pre-modern past. For Christianity is, indeed, a religion. Or, more accurately, it became a religion under the influence of the religious cultural world within which it developed. Of itself, Christianity is not that. Originally, and therefore essentially, it is the community which had formed itself around the unique figure of Jesus of Nazareth, because they recognized in him the definitive self-revelation of the fundamental wonder "God", and by virtue of this recognition orientated themselves by him and took their inspiration from Him.

The infinite good that Christianity has brought about in the world is due to this inspiration. The bad things of which it is rightly and continually accused by a scandalized modernity, have been inherited from the cultures into which it has incorporated itself in Europe. What we call Christianity or Church is, in fact, an amalgam, which means that it is the product of a cross between that original inspiration and the influences of the still unpurified European cultures.

What is the future of this amalgam "Christianity" or "Church"?

At present, this amalgam is under severe pressure in the Western world. However, it does have a future, but only on two conditions. Firstly, that it find its way back to its original inspiration, because precisely this is the source of all the good that it has brought about in the world. Secondly, that, at the same time, it free this inspiration from its mythological garb. Concretely, this means freeing itself from all that it has taken over from religion, for religion is thinking and speaking about a second world which man has thought up along the lines of this world. All that we say about that world above originates from our world here below. That is why religion has, unnoticed, attributed to the gods or to God above also much from here below that is regrettable, and in this way has condoned and even blessed the evil. That has rightly aroused aggressiveness in modern culture, which is also outraged when in Islam, for religious reasons, beheading, mutilation, whipping, intolerance, forced conversions, persecution of dissenters, slavery, discrimination against women are required or approved. But all of this has regularly been found in the history of Christianity, and modern people are now all too aware of it, so that religion, for many of them, becomes morally reprehensible.

And this can be added here: as long as, with religion, we shift the focus of life upwards, to God in heaven, we are in danger of not taking seriously enough what is within our world – reality here on earth. For a Christian this would mean failing to fulfil his task as a human being, for the inspiration coming from Jesus impels him forcefully to work for the further humanization of the world, because this is the direction in which cosmic evolution is moving. And evolution is the self-expression of the fundamental divine Wonder which is clearly striving for incarnation. There, also, lies the bridge between modern faith and unbelieving modernity. The latter has been awakened by the humanism of the 16th century and therefore insists on the absolute worth of further humanization. Where the Christian amalgam is lacking in this, modernity can only reject it. The fact that modern humanism is itself sadly lacking in this respect, as recent history shows, and remains blind to this, can only be a matter of profound regret. But anyone who lives in a glass house, like us Christians with our often hardly laudable past, should desist from throwing stones.

Conclusion

It is indispensable for us in modern times to demythologize the message of our faith. For some time now, after decades of bitter resistance, the Catholic Church has also been facing up to this task. However, it has steered clear of a very central, important area: namely, the demythologizing of the person with whom the Church in its entirety stands or falls: Jesus of Nazareth.

This person is an historical figure with all the marks of the historical. But in a pre-modern and therefore mythologically thinking culture Jesus, too, has of course been clothed in mythological garb. This book will attempt to free him of this garb, so that people in the modern era will no longer be prevented from taking him seriously. At the same time it will be shown what real qualities of the historical Jesus of Nazareth have led to his being spontaneously cloaked in myth. Precisely this is what is usually missing from the modern biographies of Jesus. They make of him a person like ourselves, which is right, because that is what he is, but unfortunately they make of him a person of the same poor evolutionary level as we are. And Jesus was not that.

The procedure in the following chapters will therefore always be to free the Jesus figure from the mythological and the unhistorical elements by which he has been surrounded. After that it will be shown what deeper and enriching vision has been concretized in those mythological notions and formulae.

CHAPTER THREE

Born of a Woman

Two events in the life of a person are beyond historical doubt: his birth and his death. We are usually much less certain about the where, the when, and the how of these two events. In this respect we have to be able to rely on credible witnesses. That applies, of course, to everything that has taken place between these two absolutely certain facts. For the life of Jesus we do have at our disposal fairly reliable witnesses. Thus we know a lot about him – at least, considerably more than about many other historical persons of the time. What are the reliable sources from which we draw this relative certainty?

Mainly the four extensive documents which, according to the scholars, were written between the years 70 and 100. They are called gospels because they announce good news (from the Greek *eu-* "good" and *angellion* "news") about Jesus. Their authors are unknown. We have their names from very questionable second-century traditions. They were, at any rate, admirers of Jesus. Together with a handful of other witnesses they teach us that he must have been born during the reign of Herod the Great, and therefore a few years before the beginning of our calendar, although this calendar dates officially from his birth. The gospels tell us furthermore that he lived in Palestine under Emperor Augustus and his successor Tiberius; that his mother was called Myriam, in Greek Maria, his father – with some question marks – Josef; that until he was 30 or 35, like his father he worked as a builder or carpenter. Afterwards, for a relatively short time (one year or three?) he traversed Galilee and Judaea as an itinerant preacher and was finally executed by the Roman governor, Pontius Pilate, in the barbaric way that the Roman judiciary executed rebels: namely, by crucifixion.

The gospel according to Mark, which must have been written after the year 70, is considered to be the oldest of the four. It says nothing at all about his birth and his childhood years. Matthew's gospel, which is dated some years later – around the year 80 – makes extensive use of Mark's text: 60 percent of his text comes from this gospel. He also used other sources: for instance, the stories about the birth of Jesus and a collection of Jesus's sayings taken from oral tradition. Some years later again, a third evangelist named Luke published a book about Jesus which took considerably less from Mark's gospel and therefore contained more material unique to this gospel. This unique material contains stories about Jesus which are peculiar to Luke's gospel, including, amongst other things, a second cycle of stories about his birth which, however, to a large extent contradict Matthew's account. Without too much trouble the three versions can be printed side by side so that, at a glance, the congruities and the contradictions are visible. For this reason these three are called the synoptics, from the Greek *syn-*: "together" and the Greek root *opt-*: "see, look". Around the year 100, a fourth gospel appears which, however, is so far removed from the synoptics – even to the point of contradiction – that its value as an historical source regarding the arrival of Jesus on the scene is very dubious.

There is almost nothing in the four gospels about the childhood of Jesus. From other sources we do know something about the education of boys in Galilee at that time. We can presuppose that much of it also applied to Jesus. Thus, for example, on the Sabbath he would have gone regularly with his parents to the synagogue where the Jewish boys could also, during the week, learn to read and write, and at the age of 12 he would certainly have taken part in Jerusalem in the pious ritual through which the young Jew became a bar-mitzwa, a "Son of the Torah"; after that he was seen as a fully-fledged Jew. Perhaps there is a connection between this and the episode related in ch.2 of Luke about the disappearance of Jesus in Jerusalem after a pilgrimage there with his parents. It is also even possible that, according to the prevailing custom, at the age of 18 or somewhat later he would have married. This does pose the question of how it comes about that, given all his travels as an itinerant preacher, absolutely nothing is said about this in the gospels.

As a boy he must also have been confronted with the horrors of that period at close hand. The town of Sepphoris was less than 10 kilometres away from Nazareth. Following the uprising led by Judas the Galilean it was completely laid waste by the Romans because of its complicity in the rebellion; 2,000 of its male inhabitants were crucified and the women and children sold into slavery. But with all of this, what do we know about him personally until his 30th year? Even the gospels tell us only what he said and did during the short period of his activity as an itinerant preacher. For everything else we have to be content with surmises. How is it to be explained that two billion people believe in this Jesus of Nazareth? The German language unfortunately lacks the possibility of showing linguistically the two very different meanings contained in the expression "believe in". It is possible in French with the two prepositions *à* and *en*, and Dutch can do it with its distinction between *aan* and *in*. "Believe in" can, in German, mean: accept the existence or the truth of something (in French *croire à*), and that is as rule not dangerous, but it does not change the world, whether for good or evil. But it can also mean: to devote oneself heart and soul to a person or a cause one deems worthy and to be prepared to involve oneself and to make sacrifices – even the sacrifice of one's own life. In French this then means *croire en*, in Dutch: *geloven in*.

This is what the profession of faith implies when it says: I believe in God, and: I believe in Jesus, the Son of God. Such a belief is clearly not without danger, but it is extremely fruitful for the world. But there can be no doubt that the faith of the great majority of Christians is scarcely more than acceptance of the historical existence of a certain Jesus, also called Christ – about 2,000 years ago –, and of his mysterious continued existence. They are often not aware that that second name contains a profession of faith which projects this simple woodworker from Nazareth out of ordinary everyday life into lonely heights.

The writer to whom we owe the oldest documents about Him, Paul of Tarsus, was unable to say anything more about Him, around the year 57, than that he was "born of a woman" – like anyone else – and was "born under the Torah", and was therefore a Jew. But birth presupposes a foetus that grows for nine months in the womb of a woman, and this foetus begins as a zygote – the result of the fertilization of an ovum by a male sperm cell. All of this happens according to the constant laws of physiology. And this is where mythology begins – understood as asserting interventions in our world coming from a supernatural world which has unlimited powers.

Mythology in the birth stories

In the first two stories about the conception and birth of Jesus – the two childhood stories in the gospels of Matthew and Luke – there is no mention of a male contribution to his conception. The necessary sexual intercourse is expressly denied in both stories. The mother of Jesus is and remains a virgin. And so for this birth it has to be a question of parthenogenesis – except that in the family of mammals, to which man also belongs, it is unthinkable. Besides, the lack of fertilization by a male sperm cell would mean that, in the zygote, the XY-chromosome pair which is constitutive of the male sex would be lacking. The foetus would only have an XX-chromosome pair which is constitutive of the female sex, and Jesus would, of necessity, have been a girl. But Jesus was definitely not a girl and his mother did not remain a virgin.

This sober conclusion will sound like blasphemy to the ears of many pious believers in the Roman and Orthodox churches. The virginity of the mother of Jesus – basically a contradiction in terms – has been so continually and intensely emphasized in Church tradition that to think otherwise about it has to be heretical. One just has to think how it is spoken about in the official liturgy, in hymn texts, in the Church's prayers, in Roman documents, in the whole Marian devotion. The liturgical texts, for example, cannot use her name without honouring her as the perpetual Mother of God. This makes an almost pathological impression.

But why this continual emphasis on the notion of virginity? Does an intact hymen have such immeasurable value? Or is sexual intercourse something reprehensible? Certainly not. But the two childhood narratives in the gospel texts are not concerned with biological, but with symbolical questions. The imagery used in the mythological language expresses the believers' conviction that the entry into world history of this completely new person Jesus is not the work of human endeavour. This Jesus is free of all that is provisional, imperfect, and disappointing in humanity. He is a pure creation of God, pure self-expression of God, and therefore a new beginning. In both of the texts about the virgin birth of Jesus, this miracle is seen in connection with the spirit of Yahweh, and so it is clear what lies beneath the mythological chalk-bed. What will be manifested later in the life of Jesus as a new humanity, a new creation, will be seen retrospectively as already present at the beginning of his existence. This insight led to the formula that he was conceived by the *ruach* or spirit of God: namely, the life-giving breath of Yahweh. In the biblical tradition the *ruach* of God is the creative force which fills the universe with life and impels it onwards. From the very beginning, therefore: completely and exclusively – according to the mythical language – the life of Jesus is marked by a spirit of renewal. This, too, is a profession of faith, but an inner-worldly one which can be affirmed also by modern thinking believers.

The "continued virginity of Mary" before, during, and after the birth of Jesus became Church dogma under massive pressure from veneration by believers. This meant that it was of no importance that Mark 6:3 and Matthew 13:55 speak of brothers of Jesus (four are named by Mark) and of sisters. Flavius Josephus also names as "the brother of Jesus" the head of the Jerusalem congregation, James, who in the year 62, by order of the High Priest Annas, was stoned to death. Despite all of this Maria remains, in the uncritical pious tradition, the virgin she once was. Tradition did, in the early days, try to come to terms with this contradiction, except that its solution is hardly convincing. These brothers of Jesus are then understood to be his cousins or his stepbrothers from a prior marriage of Joseph. Accordingly, Joseph must have been, when he married Mary, already a relatively old widower – as he is usually portrayed as a result of this lame solution.

Here, there are clearly forces at work which have nothing to do with an authentic belief in Jesus but rather with urges of a deep psychological kind – with ancient sexual taboos which made their mark even in the quite early years of the Church. Precisely because they are so deeply rooted, no opposition is to be found against the obsessive cult of the virginity of Mary. This cult, which is not based on the Bible and is thereby open to challenge, can cease only when the older generation, and with it the Marian devotion handed down through the centuries, has died out.

That is not to deny that the pre-modern, mythologically tinted devotion to Mary has offered many people secure access to the beneficial mystery that we call God. Ultimately, what we had and honoured in Mary was not an antique goddess in Christian clothing but the God who shone through this image and whom

Jesus announced, even though many pious people were not aware of it. But this kind of Marian cult has, because of the impossible dogmas (1854: The Immaculate Conception, 1950: The Assumption into Heaven), no chance of survival in critical modernity. There is also no doubt that this devotion to Mary is in rapid decline.

It is not possible to see from the accounts of Jesus's childhood who his father was. The couple of texts which treat of it are based on the fiction that it was not Joseph, the husband of Mary. In the pious tradition he is therefore never called the father of Jesus, but only his foster father, yet in the Bible fragments in which he appears – for example, in the story in Luke's gospel about the disappearance of Jesus for three days – he is, in fact, called the father of Jesus. "Your father and I have sought you sorrowing" (2:48), Mary says. Joseph and Mary are also called quite simply his parents.

The mythological element in these childhood narrations is reinforced in each of the two gospels by the intervention of mythological beings: namely, angels making proclamations. In Matthew's gospel, an angel tells Joseph to stop hesitating and to take on the role of father to the child who is about to be born; in Luke's gospel, an angel comes to Mary to urge her to declare her readiness for a mysterious conception of the Messiah.

Furthermore, what this angel says is confusing. He announces that the child will inherit the throne of his ancient ancestor David who had died 1000 years previously, although according to this pronouncement it will not be a child of David's line – who is Joseph. Expressions like "He will be a King for eternity" and "his Kingdom will have no end" (1:32-33) have no foundation in reality. There are no eternal kingships.

Use or Misuse of the Old Testament

To underpin his mythical story, Matthew, as he often does, looks to the aid of a Bible text: namely, Isaiah 7:14: "Behold, the virgin will conceive and bear a son, and his name will be called Immanuel, God with us." Some critical observations regarding these attempts at justification are necessary here. First, in general, about his procedure. It betrays a clearly mythological way of looking at the Bible. It presupposes that all texts of the Bible are "God's word" and are therefore, like oracles, infallible communications from on high. For the modern believer, that is incomprehensible for more than one reason. He can say that the fundamental miracle, God, can express Himself, reveal Himself; the fundamental miracle expresses Himself as the cosmos, and continues to do so in the history of evolution. But the modern believer cannot claim that the fundamental miracle can speak. Speaking is, namely, a purely human activity that requires a human physiology, with lungs and vocal cords and a tongue and lips. Furthermore, words (for speaking is essentially the production of words) are typically human cultural products with all the limitations and problems of understanding which human communication involves. All of that, without further ado, is then ascribed to God. Such a daring step is only possible when, with the name God, one has in mind the pre-modern *theos* in a world above – with whom the modern believer has parted company. In a nutshell, a speaking God is an anthropomorphic and therefore mythical being.

Moreover, how could one be sure that certain human words could really be communications from God? This is, indeed, what the Churches think and say about the Bible and what Islam thinks and says about the Koran, no matter how much the teachings of these books – regarded as sacred – contradict one another. But on what do these two religions base their certainty that their holy scriptures are communications from God? That is their claim, but they are unable to prove its validity. It is always a question of opinions which arise out of the depths of subjectivity, and even when one tries to give reasonable grounds for these opinions they remain opinions and personal convictions. But this kind of thing can never be convincing for other people, and so a teaching can never be confirmed by appealing to statements in a book which is held to be the word of God.

Speaking about prophecies in the Old Testament which were then supposed to be "fulfilled" in the New Testament is likewise a form of mythical thinking. One imagines that the biblical author, without knowing it himself, has predicted something that is to become reality several centuries later. Behind this is the anthropomorphic notion that God inspires in the unsuspecting biblical author what he is to write – including prophecies – with the intention of showing these as fulfilled in the New Testament, of which He Himself is the author as well. What is the point of this notion? If one can read from words in the Old Testament a hidden divine prophecy about Jesus, its so-called "fulfilment" in the New Testament confirms that the infallible authority of God puts the divine seal on what Jesus says there or does or suffers. In the tensions between those who proclaim Jesus as the divine Messiah – like the Church of Matthew – and the greater majority of the Jews who reject this claim, such "proofs" from the Bible would have had the clearly recognizable function of defending the early Church's profession of faith. When, after some time, the great majority in the Churches consisted of new members who came from Hellenistic heathenism and were not familiar with the Bible, that means of propaganda lost its force. In the gospel of Luke, who writes more for the Christians converted from heathenism, there is scarcely any trace of it.

The whole idea of two authors, one divine and one human, is pre-modern thinking and leads into a cul-de-sac. For how are the two related to one another? All attempts to define their relationship with the help of metaphors, e.g. seeing the human author as a mouthpiece or secretary or as an instrument of God, have had to be abandoned as blunders. The language of metaphor is that of images and is not a rational language. Besides, the notion of God as author presupposes the intervention of a *theos* in human activity and thereby denies the autonomy of the cosmos.

Finally, the Bible text of Isaiah 7:14 quoted above is completely unusable as an argument for the virginal conception and birth. Matthew, who wrote in Greek, uses in this case the Greek translation of the Hebrew Bible – the so-called Septuagint – produced in Alexandria in 300 BC. But the Greek translator had at that time wrongly translated the Hebrew concept "almah" – literally, young woman – as virgin. Thus the virgin birth notion is based on an error in translation. Besides, the continuation of the text says that the birth of that "Immanuel" was definitely to take place in 8 BC. It related to a political decision which King Achaz had to make at the time and not to things which would only come about some 800 years later. The Jewish scholars had already long pondered about who was meant by this Immanuel, but they had found no satisfactory answer. The result of all this was that the text was well known. Matthew applied it to Jesus. The Christian scholars were only too happy to use the authority of the Bible – which the Jews did not challenge – to show that their preaching about Jesus could appeal to the unassailable words of the Bible. But the application of this text to Jesus is a personal choice of the author, and in the Old Testament context there is not a single suggestion to warrant this application, and certainly not to the coming of the Messiah. However, Joseph Ratzinger expresses the opinion in his Jesus book that in the Bible this Immanuel definitely means Jesus. His proof works as a process of elimination. Critical examination shows, he says, that not a single child in King Achaz's circle could come into consideration. He argues from this that Immanuel has to be Jesus. But this leap has no support in logic.

Using Bible texts as conclusive proof of an opinion betrays a mythological view of the Bible. But at the same time we have the precious insight that the words of the Bible, inspired and inspiring, give direction to our lives. Yet to identify them with God's own words is a step too far. What, then, is their value? For modern believers we can say that the ultimate mystery, God, revealing Himself as the developing cosmos, is most clearly revealed in the human psyche. Persons who have a special awareness, mystically endowed natures, are able to experience more intensely than others the impulse from the ultimate mystery to achieve self-revelation. They sense, in their psyches, the need to express this in words. What these people then say is inspired human language. As human word it is provisional, so that in its current form it cannot be considered final. But in a mythologically thinking culture such an inspired word is spontaneously interpreted as the word of God coming down from heaven and therefore as an oracle: eternal, immutable, and absolute. But it is precisely not eternal and immutable. Yet insofar as it is inspired word it remains a hidden treasure – for the modern believer as well – but then in the framework of modernity. It is therefore text that never leaves the historical, inner-worldly level and does not smuggle in any supernatural elements.

The Unhistorical Character of the Two Birth Narrations

The conception of Jesus is therefore for the modern believer – despite the Bible – nothing supernatural, even if the two evangelists consciously omit the role of Joseph as father. The birth of Jesus is, then, also a normal birth. The two stories of the birth are swarming with partly mythological and partly invented, and therefore completely unhistorical details. Even the fact that there are two different and even partly contradictory accounts of the same historical event arouses suspicion. In the older of the two gospels (Matthew), the couple, Joseph and Mary, obviously live in Bethlehem, in Judaea, and so Bethlehem as the birth place of Jesus would present no problem. They have a house there (2:11) and they intend, on their return from Egypt, to settle down there again. But they don't, and they go to Nazareth without giving the slightest explanation for the choice of this scarcely known village. The reason is, of course, that Jesus is now called "Jesus of Nazareth".

By contrast, in Luke's account the couple live in Galilee, in Nazareth. But then how could Jesus be born in Bethlehem, 140 kilometres to the south. The attempt of the author to explain this is naïve: Joseph, as a descendant of David, in the town of David – Bethlehem – had to report for a census, in reality a tax declaration. Here there is a host of contradictions. At the time of Jesus's birth there was no so-called census of this kind. And, while Bethlehem is the place where David was born (according to Matthew 80 generations previously and according to Luke 40!), David left there early in his life and never returned. The genuine city of David was the fortress Jerusalem which was occupied by the Jebusites and which he captured from them. He himself designated it as the city of David (2 Samuel 5:9). Why should Joseph not have gone to Jerusalem instead? And why take Maria with him? She did not need to go. She had nothing to do with his tax declaration. What young man would, without necessity, dream of taking his highly pregnant wife on a journey of 140 kilometres on foot (or on an ass?)? It would be simply criminal. And, above all, how could an administration as efficient as the Roman one get the idea of demanding that every head of a family report in a city where his ancestor had been born 1000 years previously? Had they done that, the tax officials would certainly have found no one at home. Furthermore, if Joseph as a descendant of David was to report in Jerusalem, the same would apply to all the other male descendants of David. How many could that have been after 28 generations? An enormous number! Even David himself had 17 sons. Their names are to be found in the second book of Samuel. The whole journey to Bethlehem is therefore an invention in the service of mythology, for it only serves to show Jesus, through his birth in Bethlehem, as the long awaited Messiah, i.e. as the Saviour of the Jewish people promised by God. But with Messianism we land in mythical quicksand. It has nothing to do with historical fact, and the writer Renan was right when his first sentence was: "Jesus was born in Nazareth."

It follows, of course, that the stable and the crib are inventions of the source used by Luke. The same must be said both of the angel who announced to the shepherds the birth of the Messiah and of the choirs of angels praising God. But if the birth in Bethlehem is a myth so is the presentation of the child in the temple on the 40th day after his birth, for why would Joseph and Mary, with a baby that was only six weeks old, make a pilgrimage from Nazareth to Jerusalem – 5 days there and 5 days back – for a rite which every priest in the country could perform?

But in Matthew's account of the birth there is also nothing historical. It is true that in Babylon there were experienced astronomers, and perhaps these could read supposed religious messages from the position of the planets, perhaps even one which concerned Palestine. But is it conceivable that, after they had seen the sign in the sky, they would wait for two years before coming to Jerusalem? And is it conceivable that Herod, who panics and sees his throne endangered, would gently ask the astrologers to find this potential pretender to his throne and be good enough to tell him where he is? He would have immediately sent out his secret police to Bethlehem, which was quite near, or at least have given them to the foreigners to help with the search. And can a star (or planet or comet) stop above a particular house (for Matthew there is no stable)? If all of that is historically completely inconceivable, the story of the murder of the children and the flight into Egypt loses all credibility. Besides, the stories contradict Luke's account of the birth, where the couple do not hurry off and flee south, but on the 40th day after the birth and the presentation in the temple, calmly travel back north. The heathen philosopher Celsus, in his anti-Christian polemic, pointed out the contradiction between the two accounts. It follows from this contradiction that at least one of the accounts, though probably both, is invented – the fruit of a creative imagination.

Those are only some of the historically unsustainable elements in the two childhood stories. This being so, one can expect that creative imagination will have played a role also in other stories. The fact that something is narrated, described, and communicated by one of the evangelists is no guarantee of its reliability as history. We should certainly always ask ourselves what joyous message the evangelist has for us with his unhistorical story. In the case of the two childhood gospels it is not so difficult to discern the joyous message it contains.

The birth of Jesus is shifted from Nazareth to Bethlehem as a metaphorical statement that Jesus was the long-awaited Messiah, since according to Jewish tradition he was to be born there. The point of the Virgin Birth has been dealt with above. With the homage of the Magi, Matthew is saying that also the heathens are called to share in the salvation that begins with the Messiah, and that in this they may even occupy a position of primacy. This theme is also to be found in several of Jesus's parables. Emphasis on the star is a reminder of Bileam's prophecy in Numbers 24.17 about the prince who will be a descendant of Jacob and from whom David and his progeny, the Messiah, will be seen to spring. At the same time Matthew indicates with his story that Jesus is the new Moses, repeating what happened to Moses: threatened by Pharaoh, he will be saved from death; he comes out of Egypt into the land of Israel, bringing to it a new Torah with the promise of greater perfection. Luke, for his part, with the circumstances of Jesus's birth he has invented – stable, crib, shepherds – shows Jesus opting for the poor. Obviously, Messianic salvation is possible only on a narrow and steep path.

This analysis causes problems for the liturgy of the whole Christmas period with the feasts of the Epiphany and Candlemas. How can we honestly celebrate the coming of the Magi on 6 January and then the Flight into Egypt, the Feast of the Holy Innocents, and yet at the same time, on 2 February, the Presentation of Jesus in the temple and his return to Nazareth? And the whole highly attractive popular devotion which, in the course of the centuries, has grown up around the Holy Night with the crib and candles and Christmas Carols, loses all its foundation and turns out to be the fruit of pious fantasy.

Perhaps people will be annoyed with this analysis – not because the mind searching for truth sees errors in it, but because the inner self, needing certainty and emotional involvement, now experiences the threat of uncertainty. Be that as it may. But we should not be surprised or annoyed if modern people cannot take the stories about Jesus seriously. The accompanying danger is that Jesus himself and his message will no longer be taken seriously.

Jesus of Nazareth, (the/a) Son of God

We owe this title for Jesus to the Jewish tradition. The title "Son of God" was used as a revering acknowledgement of a person known to enjoy a special closeness to Yahweh or to be specially favoured by Yahweh. Without this history of the title in the Old Testament Jesus would probably never have been called by this name. And neither would we use this name for Him. Now we see no problem with it. But at the same time we should not forget that the Jews' notion of God is anthropomorphic, and consequently mythological, and that therefore the title is also mythological in character.

This mythological element can be reduced, to a large extent, if the Son of God is understood as the expression of an inner similarity between a person and the transcendent mystery implied in God – Son being understood as a comparison, as in the saying: "Like father, like son", which thematizes the experience that we find in a son some of the traits of his father. Naturally, we also find traits of his mother, but in the past the role of the female has always been socially undervalued – especially with regard to procreation. This only changed when von Baer discovered the ovum in 1837. Up to this point the male sperm was considered to be the only source of new life.

Thus, "Son of God" refers to someone in whom the qualities are found which are projected into God, in accordance with the image of God we have made for ourselves. If God is interpreted, with the modern believer, as fundamental Love, an encounter with someone who is utterly selfless can conjure up a comparison with God. In this sense there can be no objection to calling Jesus the Son of God because in him appears a reflection of the transcendental love that we call God. This is not our natural, everyday language. We would never call a person whom we revere "Son of God", although we might refer to him as wonderful, holy, and close to God. One can refer to Jesus as the Son of God if by that we mean: His Son in a unique way; more than the rest of us, His Son, his likeness, his image, a much richer self-revelation of the fundamental Love/God than we are.

We are only the “missing link” between Neanderthal man and what the human being is ultimately to become. Through his otherness, Jesus of Nazareth gives us an inkling of this future human being.

But the real problem with the expression “Son of God” emerges when “son” is no longer understood metaphorically – i.e. as a comparison or similarity – but genetically, as offspring, so that one slips from a symbolic understanding to an almost biological one. The extended profession of faith, the Nicene Creed, made this step in the year 325 and did not shy away from saying of Jesus that he was born of the Father before time began. And Church tradition has been doing the same ever since. It even did this afterwards in retrospect: tacitly, they interpreted the word “son” in the synoptics in the Nicaean sense. In the beginning, this could not be typographically visible the way it can be in modern languages – with the exception, unfortunately, of German. Thus Italian distinguishes between *filio* – without the initial capital letter – so that “son” has the same meaning as in the Old Testament, and *Filio* with the initial capital letter, which points to the divine status of Jesus in line with the Nicaean meaning. The oldest manuscripts of the gospels have only one kind of letter, so that it did not become clear that the synoptics were not yet attaching to the concept “Son of God” the meaning that Nicaea was to give it. They retained the same meaning as in the Old Testament. But now editions of the Bible wrongly use the capital letter for Son of God as a title for Jesus (the German editions cannot do otherwise), as if the evangelists had already thought the same as the bishops in Nicaea.

Then how was the step made from “a son of God” to “only begotten Son of God”? It probably begins with the way in which Jesus spoke of God and prayed to God: namely, with the word “Father”. He had learnt to speak and to pray like this from the Bible. With this word he expressed his attitude of perfect trust and perfect obedience to the sacred ultimate mystery which he had come to know from the Bible through the words “Lord” or “God” or “Yahweh”. Trust and obedience are precisely the two attitudes which the form of address “Father” would call to mind in the Jewish culture of his time. Jesus would not have been thinking of his lineage. In his eyes, God was not his father in fact. God was for him like a father, loving and demanding. He experienced God as love which cared but also made great demands. And this was true not only of him but also of his disciples, and so he could say: "Your father in heaven knows that you have need of all these things." (Mt 6:32) No one will, in the case of the disciples, think of God as his ontological father.

But speaking of "father" automatically summoned up the complementary concept "son", and this pair shifted slowly from the image of caring and demanding love on the one hand and dedication and obedience on the other hand to a relationship like that in a family, and thereby implicitly to a relationship of lineage. In addition to this, the use of the definite article "the" in "the Son" suggested uniqueness and even exclusivity. But Jesus included his disciples in this mutual relationship many times. In his sermon on the mount we find the expression "your father" at least 20 times.

The next step in the gradual transition from the Old Testament meaning of the term Son of God to the later Christian notion came about with John's gospel. In the prologue – completely in line with Greek philosophy – there is mention of the Logos, the intellectual self-expression of God, and also that this Logos has become flesh in the man Jesus. The combination of these two ideas – on the one hand, that the Logos originates in God, and on the other hand that Jesus is the incarnation of this Logos – paved the way to interpreting the relationship of Jesus to God as descent from God, even as his being born from God. This will lead, 200 years later, to the formulation at the Council of Nicaea that Jesus was "begotten of the Father before all ages". Thus he is the "Son of God" in a quite special and totally exclusive way – which consequently does not apply to his disciples. At the beginning of the second century the churches still believe in only one God, but in the view of the 4th evangelist (which, for a long time yet, will not be the view of many contemporary churches) Jesus is inseparably one with this one God, so that the evangelist can have Jesus say: "I and the Father are one." (10:30) He is therefore not only a son or even the son of God, but the only son – which would exclude all others from sonship in this sense. Nevertheless, the evangelist has the risen Jesus say to Mary Magdalen, quite in the manner of Jesus's speech in the sermon on the mount in Matthew's gospel: "I ascend to My father and to your father." (20:17) The doctrine about the relationship between Jesus and God is obviously not yet completely settled in John's gospel. But in any case much in this gospel indicates that it went through the hands of a series of authors – which would explain this incongruity as well.

Problems with the Nicaean Profession of Faith

But with the gospel according to John we have not yet arrived at the Nicaean formulation, which goes much further. According to the words of the Council, Jesus is not only "begotten of the Father before all ages", but he is "light from light, true God from true God, begotten, not made, of one substance with the Father". This profession of faith has become the sign of one's being authentically Christian. If we look at it more closely, what is left of this criterion if we try to reconcile faith and modernity with one another?

First, we have to give up the division of the one reality into two worlds – that of heaven and our world – so that the words of the Nicaean Creed: "He came down from Heaven and was incarnate" can no longer be entertained. Furthermore, we can no longer confirm what is endlessly proclaimed at Christmas time: "God becomes Man", as if Christmas Day were the memorable day when this happened. According to official Church teaching, Jesus is God of God not only at the point of his birth but even months earlier – even when he had begun to exist in the form of a zygote, an (as yet unfertilized!) ovum. Did God then become, at that moment an unfertilized ovum? Anyone who considers what the name God means in the Christian tradition – namely, the almighty and omniscient Creator and Master of the infinite universe – and thinks of the ovum, could only be puzzled at the joining of the two concepts God and zygote with the copula "is" or "becomes".

Moreover, how is it at all possible to *know* that a man (we are now thinking of the adult man Jesus of Nazareth) is God in the sense outlined above? We can believe it or think it. But can we *know* it? On what could any certainty be based? Certainly not, as in the past even theologians have maintained, on miracles which Jesus is supposed to have performed but which amount to the factual denial of the autonomy of the cosmos and its laws. Besides, in the Old Testament similar miracles were attributed to Moses, Elijah and Elisha, for example, and they were not incarnations of God on high. And to have recourse to the witness of other people or the Bible leads back to the initial question:

how could these "witnesses" *know* it? It could be their opinion, but in this case they would not be witnesses. And opinion is far too weak a foundation on which to build a meaningful assertion. And it is quite definite that we cannot have recourse to Jesus as witness: he never called himself, or presented himself, as God.

Furthermore, how can we conceive of the psyche of a man whose consciousness, mental horizon, ability, and notions are essentially limited, and who as God ought to be omniscient, in control of everything, capable of everything, and unlimited in every respect? Besides, the Nicaean claim that Jesus is God is in conflict with the belief of the early Church, which could not simply worship Jesus as (a) God. All who had known him and all who had heard the Church's preaching were pious Jews and therefore absolute monotheists. For them, one God beside another God or originating from another God was completely inconceivable. Looked at in this way, the Council of Nicaea has, even with the best intentions, departed from the faith of the early Church.

Here there are two things which should not be lost sight of. Firstly, that the Greek concept "dogma" only means opinion or impression – concretely, the opinion of an authority or administration which can impose its opinion on subordinates. Reliable knowledge and infallible truth are here not in the least implied. Secondly, that the Nicaean dogma did not represent the conviction of the whole Church community but only the opinion of the majority in Nicaea. The minority, following the Alexandrian presbyter Arius, saw things differently but were outvoted and finally condemned. Moreover, despite their leadership role, bishops are not the Church – still less the few hundred bishops whom the Emperor Constantine had gathered in Nicaea. Since the rediscovery of the *sensus fidelium* – the sense of faith of the believing community – we are better aware of this today.

Lex orandi, lex credendi

How did that majority in Nicaea arrive at its opinion? By interpreting a few verses of John's prologue in their own way. In those mythological days the Bible was a kind of source of oracles, the infallible word of God Himself, mostly to be taken literally. And from these few verses the majority thought they could see that Jesus really was God from God, true God from true God.

Just how open to question this interpretation was can be seen from the fact that the minority of bishops supporting Arius used exactly the same verses to defend their contrary position. Thus, for the majority, something else was at work apart from those verses from the Bible: namely, the fact that Jesus had for two centuries been worshipped like a God. This was the principle *lex orandi, lex credendi*, which formulates the conviction that the way the Church customarily prays, or the lex *orandi* – the prayer of the Church community – is also regarded as the law of faith: the *lex credendi*. This principle is itself a consequence of the conviction that the Spirit of God is active in the Church and that thereby the intuition of the faithful Church community, the *sensus fidelium*, is not mistaken.

The custom of praying to Jesus as to one God came about as ever more heathens entered the Church, coming from Hellenistic polytheism – this was at the end of the first century. For such Christians one God was something quite different from the God of the Jewish tradition. One God was a powerful being with human similarities; immortal, invisible. It was a being which did not age, which could appear and disappear at will, which listened to the prayers of its devotees and sometimes heard them, looked after them well and could even give them eternal life. For Christians coming from heathenism it was clear that all of this applied to the glorified Jesus much more than to all the deities they had once worshipped. They had absorbed that polytheistic image of God with their mother's milk and it still influenced them even when they had come to believe in the God of the Bible. And so it came about that in churches from Syria to Spain it was no problem for them to pray to Jesus as to (a) God and at the same time – also with no problem – to use the Bible and the language of prayer rooted in it to worship the one true God of the biblical tradition.

Only in the 3rd century, when Greek philosophical thought was gaining ground in the churches, did it become clear that simultaneous worshipping of Jesus-God and Yahweh-God was problematic and that a solution to the problem had to be found. Up to the end of the 3rd century all kinds of solutions were suggested, defended, criticized, corrected, rejected as unsatisfactory. Early in the 4th century – the Church had in the meantime acquired legal status under Constantine – the discussions became less and less friendly and eventually ended in hostile polemic and reciprocal condemnations. Finally the Emperor, concerned about the unity of the Roman Empire which was coming under severe pressure along its borders, intervened with force. In his summer palace in Nicaea on the north coast of Asia Minor, in the year 325, he called together the church leaders of the whole empire to make them arrive at a binding solution to the theological problem and in this way to bring an end to the division. Only a very modest number of bishops came to Nicaea – some 200 to 300.

On the basis of the widespread custom, now two hundred years old, of praying to Jesus as to a God, the majority concluded that he really was God. But this majority clearly did not see that they were using the one word "God" at the same time with two distinct meanings: one was the Jewish, monotheistic meaning, and the other the Hellenistic, polytheistic meaning. This was partly due to the fact that there is no indefinite article in Greek, so that the difference between "God" and "a God" did not become clear. And, as we have said above, only one kind of letter was used in the Bible manuscripts, so that it was also visually impossible to discern whether with the word *theos* the one God was meant or a God.

The Council did achieve the unity sought by Constantine, but in a way which was not in accord with the gospels: namely, by forcing the minority, with the help of Imperial sanctions, to accept the opinion of the majority as Divine truth. Those who did not obey – the minority around Arius – were hunted out of the Church as heretics. Thus only the majority, with their opinion, remained and the conflict within the Church seemed to be over.

It seemed to be over, but it was not. It would take three more councils, from 325 to 451, to achieve this, and in the course of the 125 years many hundreds of thousands of devout Christians would, on the basis of theological differences of opinion and misunderstandings, be condemned by whoever was the majority and excluded from the Church of Jesus Christ. In the Council of Constantinople in 381, not only was the teaching of Nicaea confirmed, but at the same time all those who did not want to maintain that the Spirit of God was the third Divine person were condemned. In the turbulent Council of Ephesus in 431, the devout Nestorius was condemned because, while he accepted that Jesus was both God and man, he could not accept that Mary should therefore be called the Mother of God. She was, quite simply, the mother of Jesus. The majority, led by Bishop Cyril of Alexandria, judged, on the contrary, that Mary could indeed be called the Mother of God. In fact, she ought to be so called. With subtle philosophical arguments about two natures in the one person of Jesus the Council came to the conclusion that anyone who did not agree was to be considered a heretic. Thus Nestorius and his followers became heretics and had to experience in their own flesh what that meant. Since then, "Mother of God" became the normal title for the mother of Jesus.

Before peace came at last, yet another heresy, that of Eutyches, was to be condemned in 451 at the Council of Chalcedon, the last of the four great dogmatic councils. Eutyches taught that Jesus of Nazareth was God to such an extent that no independent human nature could any longer be attributed to Him. It was as if his divine nature had absorbed his human nature. This meant that Mary deserved the title Mother of God still more than had been thought at Ephesus. But the Council thought this opinion was going too far, and the views of Eutyches were condemned as heretical. Today's Copts in Egypt are the spiritual descendants of the group expelled on that occasion: the Monophysites.

These incessant wranglings and condemnations which took place in the course of the century that followed the Council of Nicaea reveal the fact that there must have been a basic error in the ideas of the majority at Nicaea. What this error was has been shown above. Despite this fundamental error, the opinion of the majority became dogma – no longer as an opinion held by some legal authority but as binding truth. It even became the foundation of an infallible Church doctrine, a questionable foundation which today is beginning to crumble under the pressure of modern insights.

This gives us, here at the end of this chapter, a provisional answer to the question posed in the title of the book: Jesus of Nazareth, a person like us? Yes. Despite the solemn declaration of faith in Nicaea and Constantinople, he is no mythological God-Man, no alien from outside the cosmos who has come down to us. But this is only a provisional answer. It has still to be subject to further differentiation.

However, not only the birth of Jesus, but also his public appearance in that one year (or was it three?) described by the evangelists, was soon veiled in the fog of mythology. This is dealt with in the next chapter.

CHAPTER FOUR

From his Baptism to his Death

What we know about the time between the birth of Jesus and his early death is based, as has been said, almost exclusively on the four little books from the years 70 to 100, called gospels because they announce the gospel of Jesus Christ, literally: the "good tidings", the joyful message about Jesus, the Christ or Messiah. A large part of the content, at least in the three older gospels, is clearly historical, not mythological, because it concerns exclusively our human world. Thus we can read this part without the danger of running aground in mythology.

But historical in the sense of "not mythological" does not necessarily imply a guarantee of reliable reporting, a more or less accurate recording of past events. The non-mythological sections can also contain legends or wisdom in the form of stories. In the Old Testament several books of the Bible, such as Esther or Judith or Tobias belong to this category. To be able to speak of historical in the broad sense, as is the case with the concept of the "historical novel", it is sufficient that no power outside the cosmos intervenes in the workings of our own world. Where in the gospels such a force is seen as intervening, we are dealing with mythology. In this sense a whole series of stories about Jesus are mythological, especially where he is seen as a faith healer or exorcist. In these cases the reader should always ask: What does the evangelist intend by his narration? For he is never telling fairy tales. He is always bringing good news about Jesus. This remains so, even when he himself believes in the reality of his story, although that is scientifically not tenable. And it is quite likely that this is mostly the case. He was a man living in an age which thought in a mythological way. He believed in a God above, Who intervened at will and for Whom nothing was impossible. But what was important for him was not the story itself, but its significance for our salvation, worked by this Jesus who appears in the story. He has not been a witness of the events he related. He wrote down what after Jesus' death his disciples had told about him and had been conserved in the oral tradition. And also his disciples considered that for God nothing was impossible.

It would be a waste of time to try and test the many individual stories to uncover their mythological component. We have to accept from the outset that Jesus again and again appears in a mythological context, for the authors thought so and that added spontaneously a mythological colouring to their otherwise historical narratives. This did not necessarily destroy their historicity, but it did often clearly weaken it. What follows will only deal with the miracle stories in the three synoptic gospels. The fourth gospel will for the time being be omitted. The reason for this will become clear later.

In what follows this principle will everywhere be applied: what today is no longer conceivable, because it contradicts the laws of nature, can neither have happened in the past. Where the gospels narrate such things about Jesus, we have either to consider them as products of the imagination typical of their era, or as a mythological representation and interpretation of real facts. Otherwise, Jesus loses his human quality and is no longer real. And what do we gain by a Jesus who is not real?

But the evangelist is essentially the announcer of a message which should enrich our lives in a palpable way. How then can we as modern people read of the miracles attributed to Jesus in the three synoptic gospels in such a way that they appear as an enriching message? These miracles are his exorcisms, his healings, his awakenings of the dead and his so-called nature miracles: the calming of a storm, two multiplications of the loaves, his walking on water. Also the transfiguration on the mountain could be included here. Only after that will the miracle stories in the fourth gospel, the gospel according to John, be considered.

The Exorcisms

Mark often speaks of Jesus driving out evil spirits. He has no problem with it. For him, as for all of his contemporaries, evil spirits are real beings. Even for many of our seemingly modern contemporaries devils have a kind of reality. But because they must belong to a world other than our scientific world – our laws of nature indeed do not seem to affect them – for modern man they are mythological interpretations of natural processes in the human subconscious without any corresponding reality outside the cosmos. If Jesus is brought into that mythological world he also becomes a mythological figure. It is certain that the evangelists, just like the entire Jewish community, believed in the reality of devils and possession by them. Also in the Acts of the Apostles expressions of such belief are to be found, as in 8:7, 16:18 and 19:13-17. In a pre-modern and therefore superstitious climate, in which the devil is an invisible humanlike figure and is able to take hold of a person, it is easy to see him at work. We need only to think of the Middle Ages, in which the devil was even a morbid obsession, one of the worst results of which was witch hunting.

More than once the exorcism has to do not with individual cases and personal destinies, but with groups. For example Mark 1:39: "He preached in the synagogues and drove out demons", or in 3:11-12, after there is mention of many healings: "When those possessed by impure spirits saw Him, they fell down before him and cried: "You are a son of God." And two verses further on he gives his disciples the power to drive out devils themselves, which according to 6:12 they do indeed. In 3:23-27 he even explicitly defends his expulsion of devils against the calumnies of his opponents. This excess of powerful acts in relation to mythological beings requires an explanation. In the modern world only psychic disturbances show a similarity with those cases of possession. But were so many people psychically disturbed in those days? With the frequency and universality of these phenomena Mark clearly wanted to show his readers that the presence of Jesus in the world essentially meant a victorious battle with the forces of evil which reject God and harm man and which are active everywhere in the world. In any case, precisely in this way Jesus (or the early tradition) defends in Mark 3:22-30 his exorcisms against the blasphemies of his foes: they show that God, through Him, sets up his kingdom in Israel and in the world.

But because in Mark's gospel the driving out of devils is often closely associated with healings, possession must have something to do with sickness. As early as 1:32 we read: "All the sick and the possessed were brought to him (...) and he healed many (...) and drove out many demons." Sometimes the exorcism has explicitly to do with healing, more specifically with the healing of a mental illness. Perhaps this is not immediately obvious in 1:23-27, when right at the beginning of his activity as preacher, Jesus in the synagogue in Capharnaum drives an "impure spirit" out of someone, but some indications suggest that also there we can think of this person as a psychiatric patient. A quite clear case is the healing in chapter 5 of the possessed man of Gerasa. And when the demon was driven out of the little daughter of the Syrophoenician woman (7:29), Matthew says explicitly that the girl was healed. Also the epileptic deaf and dumb boy in 9:17-29 is healed, when he is saved from a deaf and dumb spirit. Of course, in the eyes of modern man all of this belongs to the domain of mythology.

In pre-modern times every unusual thing that was inexplicable and frightening was spontaneously seen as linked to the power of the devil, for in the Book of Genesis God Himself saw and said that everything He had made was very good. Thus, suffering and sickness were not part of God's plan and had to be the work of his enemy who, at night, had sown weeds in God's field. This applied especially to attacks of hysteria and epilepsy or when someone clearly suffered from mental disturbances, and his actions and speech had largely lost their human character. The devil must have had a hand in these things. With the healing of the boy in Matthew 17:15 the father explicitly talks of epilepsy, but Mark, who is Matthew's source, speaks just as explicitly of possession by the devil. And it is clear that the possessed man from Gerasa in Mark 5 suffers from a serious mental disturbance and is healed by his encounter with Jesus. The moving of a legion of devils into 2000 swine, which concludes the narration, is quite clearly a product of popular imagination. Because, in the eyes of the Jews, pigs were unclean animals, their herd seemed to be an obvious place for the crowd of impure spirits driven out by Jesus to flee to.

What are we, as modern people, to think of all of these disconcerting stories, and what are the consequences for our faith in Jesus? The answer is linked to the question of what we are to think about his acts of healing. The expulsions of devils by Jesus are clearly just the contemporary mythological interpretation of his acts of healing, an interpretation we should forget. And so we should ask: are those healings by Jesus credible? If the answer is yes, then the bizarre stories about possession and liberation from it have meaning for the modern believer, but they must, of course, then be interpreted as mental and psychosomatic healings which are presented by the evangelists in mythological garb.

Jesus as Faith Healer

One must not be still living in the Middle Ages or thinking in a mythological way to admit that certain people have the gift of activating autogenic forces in a sick or suffering person, usually by the laying on of hands, in such a way that recovery is achieved without the use of Western or Eastern medicine. A collective also seems capable of this. In his book *The Perennial Philosophy*, Aldous Huxley, who was not at all involved with the Church, considers it very probable (and this applies, for example, to Lourdes) that the psychic forces which are awakened by the intense religious faith of thousands can charge the surrounding atmosphere with a kind of spiritual energy in such a way that, there too, sometimes unexplainable healings take place. That this is no empty fantasy is shown by the report of the then completely agnostic doctor Alexis Carrel, who later won the Nobel Prize for medicine, about the cure in Lourdes of one of his own patients, which took place under his very eyes. For believers, this cure was an authentic intervention from the all-powerful otherworld, and thus a miracle. For him it was just a puzzle, something temporarily inexplicable, with which he grappled over a long period of time. And so one and the same event can be interpreted in more than one way.

Hence the question is forced upon us: was Jesus perhaps a faith healer, a wonder doctor? Did he have innate or acquired paranormal powers? To make the stories of his performance as a healer feasible without having recourse to the intervention of a supernatural and therefore mythological power for which supposedly nothing is impossible, reference is often made to other faith healers from antiquity, like Apollonius of Tyana in the 1st century. Although reliable philological studies place question marks over most of the cures related about him, there are still some left which seem to have a basis in reality. But for us the important question is not whether there have been other nature healers, people endowed with unusual natural powers, but whether Jesus was such a one. And that is an important question, for if he was not, are we not being led astray by the gospels? For we pray and meditate then about invented stories which have merged together from all kinds of anonymous little sources, erroneously thinking that we are dealing with events which could teach us who the real Jesus was, how he behaved, what he did, and what he taught. These stories acquire then a halo of importance and truth, and what Jesus says and does in them becomes the norm for our behaviour. But what we are getting to know in reality is not Jesus but only the rich fantasy of unknown narrators. What then can we make of these narratives? We don't read them because they are excellent stories, but because we want to get to know Jesus. Hence we are faced with the challenge of looking further at the problem of the cures performed by Jesus.

What then is true in these stories and reports of cures? Are the evangelists conjuring up for us an image of Jesus which they have thought up (or that had been thought up by the oral tradition on which their gospels are based) and are they guilty perhaps of false propaganda to win over their readers for Jesus? First we must examine what they tell us about the cures performed by Jesus. Again we start our investigation from the gospel according to Mark, which is the source of most of the reports about cures related by Matthew and Luke.

Not only the exorcisms but also the cures are presented by Mark sometimes in a more or less global manner. In 1:34 we read: "In the evening they brought all the sick and the possessed to Jesus (...) and he healed many suffering from all possible illnesses, and he cast out many devils." Something similar is found in 3:10 and in 6:56: "And always when he entered a village or a town they laid the sick in the streets and besought him that they might touch the hem of his garment. And as many as touched him were made whole." Unexplainable cures effected by the laying on of hands can be acceptable, because today also nature healers seem to have this paranormal gift. But to believe in cures as if on an assembly line, without any laying on of hands, sometimes with the sick person merely touching a piece of cloth, that is asking too much of a critical mind.

Fortunately, in the gospels we are dealing mostly with individual cures. Apart from the ones presented as exorcisms, we can cite from Mark's gospel: the healing of Peter's mother-in-law in 1:30, of a leper in 1:42, of a lame man in 2:11-13, of a man with a withered hand in 3:5, of the daughter of Jairus in 5:41-42 in connection with the cure of a woman suffering from an issue of blood in 5:28-29, of the daughter of a Syrophoenician woman in 7:26, of a blind man in Bethsaida in 8:23-25, and of a second blind man in Jericho in 10:51-52.

At some of these healings Jesus does nothing at all, but merely speaks. A couple of times he even heals from a distance, as in the case of the little daughter of the Syrophoenician woman. In dealing with the woman who has an issue of blood, he does feel as if a force went out from Him. But there is no question here of a transfer of energy through the laying on of hands. This makes it difficult to accept that these and the other healings are historical facts. An intervention from God on the other hand would make the healing activity of Jesus as a whole mythological and therefore no longer real. And that would make Jesus himself unreal for us.

Sometimes one could suspect that a psychosomatic type of cure is the historical kernel of a story of recovery, which afterwards, for the purposes of preaching, was revised and enriched: the sick person was so full of despairing hope that the force of his desire activated the energies slumbering in his organism, and these then prompted the beginning of a healing process. We could perhaps think of this in the case of the woman cured of the issue of blood. This could also perhaps explain why Jesus, after he cured the blind man in Jericho, says in Mark 10:52: "Thy faith hath made thee whole." "Faith" would then point to the man's yearning and confidence in the powers of recovery and in Jesus' willingness to cure him. But perhaps there is a better explanation.

For what did the evangelists intend with their stories of cures? Did they want to communicate historical facts? They were not chroniclers and still less reporters. They were announcers of good news. And this good news was not that Jesus of Nazareth at that time had healed some people of one illness or another. What would their readers half a century later gain from this for their own lives? Nothing. But they did gain very much from this good news: during his life a healing force came from Jesus to all who turned to him in confidence and asked to be cured; without any doubt after his death he would remain so for all who turned to him. No longer healing in the physical sense, but more deeply, truly, existentially. He would make new human beings of them. The completely legendary or half legendary tales of healing were for them images of the real salvation which, even after his death, came from the unity with him. Naturally that presupposed their conviction that death had not wiped out Jesus, but had instead transferred him into a richer form of existence. The stories about his driving out devils and about cures are, in other words, confessions of faith in his Resurrection. This will be dealt with more in detail in Chapter Six.

The stories of healing, therefore, need to be seen as symbolical. They are in no way reliable reports about the historical doings of Jesus, but are confessions of faith of the primitive Church. As symbolical stories they can also be freely invented, just as the parables Jesus uses are not based on historical facts. He is only concerned with the deeper meaning of his stories. The Greek original of the healing of the blind man in Jericho (Mark 10:52) says literally: "Your faith has saved you." And faith means here something other than what it means in the psychosomatic explanation above. The concept takes on the meaning in which it is again and again used in the Bible, often enough in connection with the concept of salvation. With this concept not a transitory physical healing is meant, but a spiritual well-being, lasting beyond death. It is as if the evangelist is playing two manuals at the same time. He seems to be speaking about the transitory healing as the fruit of an intensive faith in the healing powers of the miracle doctor Jesus. But in fact and even primarily he is thinking of our lasting health, our existential salvation and completion through our turning to Jesus, i.e. through faith in him.

The synoptic evangelists give no indication that they understand the cures in a symbolic sense. On the contrary, they give the impression that they are communicating real medical facts, which show what Jesus was able to do and who he was. In any case, the symbolic interpretation is the only way in which the preacher can speak plausibly today to the modern thinking believer about Jesus' healings and exorcisms. And in this he finds an ally in the fourth evangelist, who undoubtedly understands the cures as symbols, as we shall see. Given this support, it is conceivable that the synoptic evangelists at least tacitly think the same, although their words quoted above: "Your faith has saved you" are the only signal of this.

That the evangelists have given in their gospels a surprising amount of space to the healing activity of Jesus, can perhaps be explained in the following way. The worship of Jesus in the primitive Church became gradually more intense, and the tendency to elevate and glorify him became ever stronger. In every culture that thinks in a mythological way, the excellence of a revered person is spontaneously highlighted by attributing to him all kinds of extraordinary achievements. For the primitive Church Jesus was the long-awaited Messiah, and so he must have done the extraordinary things which were expected of the Messiah. This included also what, according to Luke 4:17-21, Jesus himself had said in his programmatic speech in Nazareth. He had quoted there Isaiah 61:1-2 and had added to the words of the prophet only that the blind would see. But in Matthew 11:5, in his answer to John the Baptist, who seems to doubt his Messianic mission, he enumerates all kinds of cures which are reported everywhere in the gospel. The idea was that, since all of that was expected of the Messiah, Jesus also must have done it. The evangelist then provided the necessary substantiating stories.

It is also very probable that the oral tradition or the evangelist found some of these stories in a pool of miraculous stories circulating within Hellenistic culture. But Jesus had also thought up stories himself. Some of the parables are of this kind. John Dominic Crossan, in his book *The Power of Parable*, summarizes the development thus: "Fiction by Jesus became fiction about Jesus." The evangelists were simply following his example. At the same time, the cures were to deliver convincing proof of his Messianic dignity, as an answer to the scandal that God's Messiah, the Saviour, instead of ruling from a kingly throne, had ended wretchedly on a cross.

Criticism of the stories of healing can therefore be summed up as follows: even if their untraceable roots were to have been historical, the way they have been presented is certainly not. This presentation is purely mythological, since what is impossible or highly improbable is tacitly presented as possible and real as a result of God's intervention through the person of Jesus. The evangelists obviously had no problem with this kind of mythology.

What is noticeable in the stories of cures is the suddenness with which they happen. Nowhere do we see the (normal) gradual transition from sickness to health. Convalescence is an unknown quantity in the gospel. Only on one occasion does a cure require two steps (Mark 8:23-25). This suddenness renders the stories of cures still more suspect. It reminds us of the likewise improbable suddenness of the decision to give up everything and follow Jesus, as it is described in the case of the calling of the first disciples at the Lake of Gennesaret (Mark:18-

20) or of the calling of Levi (Mark 2:14). That is not really the way the human psyche functions. But with this suddenness both of the healing and of the decision to follow Jesus Mark highlights Jesus's absolute superiority.

The Nature Miracles in the Synoptic Gospels

But along with the exorcisms and cures, the gospels include some stories of miracles which have to be regarded as pure inventions, because they completely contradict the laws of nature. These are the so-called nature miracles. They make Jesus seem unreal, because he looks like a completely mythological character. Amongst these are: Jesus calms a storm (Mark 4, Matthew 8, Luke 8), walks on the water (Mark 6, Matthew 14), with five loaves of bread and two fish he gives so much food to 5,000 men (plus, of course, a crowd of women and children) that at the end twelve baskets of pieces of bread are left over (Mark 6, Matthew 14, Luke 9), and in Mark 7 and Matthew 15 he even does it again, this time with 4,000 men and an unnamed number of women and children. It is as clear as day that these stories are completely irreconcilable with the laws of physics.

Nevertheless, the evangelists took them to be facts. Influenced by a world view in which nothing is impossible for God, they had no reason to doubt the reality of their narratives. But we, educated as we are in the clear certainty that there are unshakable laws of nature, can only see them as mythological creations. The question is not where these stories came from. As has been said above, in Hellenism there existed a pool of miracle stories about great men. The question is only why the evangelists chose these particular stories. The answer is: because they are visual confessions of faith. With powerful images they wanted to illustrate that in Jesus the unlimited activity of God was being made visible. Anyone who reads them with the Old Testament in the back of his mind, can hear in them the clear echo of verses which ascribe to the power of Yahweh what Jesus is doing there. Walking on the water is reminiscent of Job 9:8: "Only Yahweh can walk across the waves of the sea." The calming of the storm reminds us of Psalm 107:23-32; and with the reaction of the disciples in the boat: "Who is this whom even the wind and the waves obey?" the evangelist himself is suggesting the connection with this Psalm.

In the two nature miracles which are associated with the lake, possibly something still deeper is hidden. The Jewish people were not a nation of seafarers like the Greeks and the Phoenicians. For them the sea was a dangerous force, a threat, the embodiment of the powers of evil, the symbol of death. In the Book of Daniel chapter 7 the four terrifying animals emerge from the sea, and in the Apocalypse chapter 21 we read that in the new world there will no longer be any sea. In the two stories Jesus shows himself the lord of the waters, as he strides masterfully over the lake and closes its greedy jaws once and for all: he is victorious over evil and death. That explains why Mark, with the calming of the storm (4:39) and with the first exorcism (1:25), both of which illustrate equally the victorious power of Jesus over evil, has him use exactly the same powerful word of command which, translated literally, would be: “Be muzzled”.

The multiplication of the loaves is, of course, reminiscent of the manna in the desert in Exodus 16:13-15. The three synoptic gospels relate the multiplication simply as a fact and without commentary. They leave it to the reader to see more in the stories. But they lead him to a deeper reading by narrating Jesus’ deed in the context of caring for the people in a difficult situation. Here Mark sees Jesus as the shepherd who is concerned with the fate of sheep without a shepherd (6:34), who cures them, encourages them with his good tidings, and in the end gives them ample food, so that they do not collapse on their journey. A few details which of themselves are completely superfluous to the story, namely, that the people are to sit down and form groups of 50 and 100, and Jesus’ gesture before he begins distributing the food, show in the background of the activity the celebration of the Eucharist in the early Church. In this way Mark discreetly indicates what he has in mind when he tells the story of the multiplication of the loaves.

The nature miracles are in no way historical reports. There is also no sense in looking for an historical stratum underneath them, even though this might be a temptation for a preacher who is irritated by the factual impossibility of what he reads out. With regard to the multiplication of the loaves, for example, the explanation is sometimes given that Jesus starts off a chain reaction when he distributes his own evening meal (really that of the 12 disciples). Suddenly all produce their evening meal, which up to this point they have kept well concealed, and share it with their neighbours. For the careful reader of the text, this attempted explanation is shown not only to have no foundation, but to be completely blind to what the evangelist wants to teach us: namely, that the connection with Jesus gives life and fulfilment.

The best explanation of the nature miracles is probably that they are an attempt to interpret the mysterious depth we sense in Jesus by tracing it back to its source: the mighty presence of God in Him. Anyone who wants to treat the stories as an account of real events – and there are still pious people who do it – reduces the meaningful multiplication of the loaves, the calming of the storm and the victorious walking of Jesus over the lake, which is an image of the Resurrection, to a magical trick

Neither of the two raisings from the dead in the synoptic gospels are mythological tricks of magic performed by Jesus. Of the twelve-year-old little daughter of Jairus he says himself that the girl is not dead but is asleep, meaning that she is in a kind of coma. He will wake her out of this coma. This brings us back to the cures dealt with above. Eugen Drewermann gives a rich interpretation of this story, based on depth psychology: the girl is 12 years old, is on the threshold of adulthood since a Jewish girl was marriageable at 12 years of age. But she does not dare to take the step to adulthood and flees into the unconscious. Jesus helps her to cross this threshold, so that she can lead a normal life.

The case of the young man from Naim must have been a case of apparent death, and the return to life a reawakening from this state. This is again a cure. Naturally the bystanders interpret this as an intervention from on high. They believe that from there come all unexpected good things (also all unexpected distressing things). The modern believer does not see it like this anymore. But why does Luke tell this story, which is found only in his gospel? Surely not to depict Jesus as a miracle healer or magician, but to highlight the life-renewing power that emanated from Jesus and which – and this is the most important thing – still emanates from Him. We must continually remind ourselves that an evangelist is one who announces good tidings and is not an historian or journalist. What he wants to tell is not what Jesus did in those days, in which case he would be a reporter, but the liberating, saving role he continually plays in the life of the believer. Ultimately he reminds us in the language of imagery of the resurrection of Jesus himself. Chapter Six will deal with this in detail.

There remain a few more stories which run counter to that which in the light of modern thinking we consider possible: the transfiguration of Jesus on the mountain (Mark 9, Matthew 17, Luke 9), his cursing of a fig tree (Matthew 21:19) which makes the tree completely wither within a few hours, and the order he gives Peter in Matthew 17:27 to go fishing and to open the mouth of the first fish he catches, to find there the double silver piece that the collector of temple tax requires of himself and Peter.

We can suspect that the historical kernel of the transfiguration was an experience the disciples of Jesus had, when they saw on one occasion that while he was praying, his face began to shine and they remembered what was told about Moses in Exodus 34:29: namely, that light radiated from his face after his encounter with God on Mount Sinai. The account in the gospels is the mythological treatment of this kernel in the oral tradition. The appearances of Moses and Elijah show the mythological character of the story. The cloud and the voice from the sky further reinforce this character. This transfiguration is therefore another profession of the faith that in Jesus one experienced the presence of God.

With regard to the fish with the silver coin in its mouth: this fish is a popular motif in the literature of antiquity, well known because of the story of the ring of Polycrates. Here it serves to highlight the unique relationship between Jesus and God. The context of the cursing of the fig tree shows that this is a symbolic narration, a kind of parable, in which Matthew arbitrarily interprets the destruction of Jerusalem as a consequence of the rejection of Jesus' message by the Jewish leadership. In many places in his gospel we can trace Matthew's aggressive attitude towards the great majority of the Jewish people, who thought it was a reprehensible error to see in Jesus the long-awaited Messiah and who therefore banned from their synagogues as apostates those who had become Christian. This aggressive stance often misled Matthew to make statements which were unjust to the Jewish people as a whole.

Symbolism in John's Gospel

John, and he alone, ascribes to Jesus a third raising from the dead, which is the best known and the most spectacular one in the whole Bible: the raising of Lazarus. Despite the impression of historical reality which the story gives by virtue of its concrete and lively character, it is from beginning to end a purely fictitious creation of the author. That it is freely invented is immediately clear from its sheer impossibility. The human brain, after being deprived of oxygen for a quarter of an hour, collapses completely and irreversibly. This causes all vital functions to cease once and for all. And Lazarus was already dead for three full days. His sister even said that one could smell the decay. Anyone who after all of this is prepared to accept the raising of Lazarus as fact is still living in a far-off pre-scientific past.

Perhaps the fourth evangelist himself still believed in the reality or at least the possibility of this resurrection. But that was not the reason for telling that story. What he wanted to say was that no person can be so dead and lost – "dead" not understood here in the biological sense – that Jesus cannot call him back to life – "life" also not understood here in the biological sense. Lazarus's emerging from the tomb when Jesus called his name, shows this with intensely vivid imagery.

As with the other nature miracles, John explains also with regard to this miracle the richly symbolical meaning of his story: for the believer Jesus is the source of life and resurrection (v.25-26). The fact that the raising of Lazarus is a symbolical story, freely invented by the author, and not the report of an event, is further reinforced by the fact that Lazarus is not a historical figure. In the whole of the New Testament his name occurs only in this episode. He is not even mentioned when Jesus (according to Luke) comes to eat with Martha and Mary, and Mary to the annoyance of her sister entertains Jesus. Yet John refers to him here as their beloved brother and as an intimate friend of Jesus. He even has Jesus weeping at his grave – very strange indeed, since he is immediately going to see him alive again. Finally, if this raising from the dead was a historical fact, this sensational miracle would have been known in all the churches and it would certainly have left clear traces in the synoptic gospels, which were written before John and therefore were closer to the narrated event. But whereas all three dealt in detail with the much less spectacular raising of the little daughter of Jairus, there is no mention at all of the raising of Lazarus.

The last nature miracle is the changing of water into wine in Cana. Just as much as the previous miracle, this one leaves the inescapable impression that Jesus belongs to the world of mythology and therefore cannot be taken seriously. And just like the raising of Lazarus, the wine miracle is also found only in John. This already arouses suspicion. None of the synoptic evangelists knows of it. Moreover an abundance of stories in the Hellenistic East circulated about water changing into wine. In addition, the calling of the first disciples, which precedes the wine miracle, is completely at variance with the version presented in the synoptics, where it takes place at the Lake of Galilee, and the four men called there are fishermen, whereas John has it take place at the Jordan, in Judaea, where there would be no talk of boats and nets.

The story of the wine miracle is inconceivable also for other reasons. Firstly, there is the chemical impossibility of changing, without some kind of manipulation, pure H^2O into a drink with 12 percent alcohol. Such a conversion would turn the whole of science upside down. Secondly, there is another inconceivable element in the story. If it was a question of giving the wedding guests, who had already had plenty to drink, the possibility of drinking on merrily, one single 100-litre barrel would already have been far too much. But no, it was to be, according to the story, 600 litres. The staff would therefore have to draw 600 litres of water, in jugs and buckets, from the village well. That would have meant innumerable trips back and forth and, even if the well had not been very far away, such an undertaking would have taken an eternity. In the meantime the guests were waiting for wine, as was the man in charge of the meal, who saw how his staff ran in and out with jugs and buckets, although he had not hired them for this purpose. Is it conceivable that he would not have intervened?

These impossible elements in the story prove that the author's meaning was purely symbolical. The abundance of precious wine should open the reader's eyes to the richness and blessing that the appearing of Jesus meant for the whole of humanity. This is also suggested by Jesus' reference to "his hour", which for John always includes both his death and his resurrection. Augustine of Hippo points to this meaning with a profound answer to the question what was done with that abundance of excellent wine that remained after the wedding: "We are still drinking from it."

Whereas the synoptic evangelists tell the story of the multiplication of the loaves without commentating on it, John strives throughout the whole of chapter 6 to shed light on its deeper meaning and to explain the symbolical value of this story, although as a man belonging to a pre-modern culture he will have had no problem in accepting that it really happened. He is not interested in the multiplication of the loaves in itself, as a magical act or a miracle, he is only interested in its deeper meaning, and this deeper meaning is the only reason why he tells the story. The meaning is eucharistic. The whole of Jesus' speech, which takes up nearly the whole of chapter 6, is a sermon by the evangelist about the meaning of the eucharistic gatherings of the faithful. A rich and inspiring sermon, no doubt. But everything in this sermon is his own personal opinion, and there is nothing in it that binds us, any more than our personal opinions would bind him. These verses cannot, therefore, be used as dogmatic statements, as if they were the very words of a man who was also God. Anyone who uses them as such a foundation is building on sand. If the reader thinks he has good reasons to forget them, he can quietly do that. That is good advice when we come to the in essence brutal verses 53-56b, which require that we eat the flesh of Jesus and drink his blood. Can such words really be said to Jewish listeners, for whom drinking blood was declared an abomination by God?

John relates two further cures. That they are impossible is as clear as day. The first is the healing, in chapter 9, of the man born blind. Someone who has never had sight cannot suddenly see. He must first learn to convert into cohesive, meaningful images the thousand light impulses which stimulate his retina. This process precisely is what is meant by "seeing". This process takes time. That is why it takes so long before a baby really sees. The second healing is the healing in chapter 5 of the lame man who for 38 years was lying beside the pool of Bethesda. When someone has not used his leg and thigh muscles for such a long time they have shrunk to such an extent that there can be no question of his standing up and "going off with his bed". To do that he would need a long treatment by physiotherapists.

But John himself emphasizes through the words added by Jesus, that he interprets the two healings symbolically, as pointing at something else. The healing of the lame man is a sign that God is at work through Jesus (5:17-19). Even more explicitly he emphasizes the symbolic meaning of the cure of the man born blind in 5:29-40. This cure shows, in an image, that the encounter with Jesus opens our eyes for the truth of faith and is thereby salutary.

The I-Am Words in John's Gospel

The gospel according to John is undoubtedly the least historical of the four. The main reason is not that it is 70 years or more distant from what is narrated and written about the year 100, as is generally assumed by biblical scholars. The main reason is that in John's gospel Jesus uses a completely different language from that used in the three synoptics. In these he only rarely draws his listeners attention to himself. Again and again he directs their attention to God or to their fellow human beings. Only exceptionally, as in the well-known passage from Matthew 11:27-30, does he speak somewhat in the style of John: "All things are delivered to me by my Father" and "Take up my yoke upon you and learn from me". Or in Luke 11:31: "And behold more than Solomon is here." With such words he underlines his own crucial importance. But by doing so he confronts us with difficult questions regarding his self-consciousness. Where, in this affirmation of his importance, is the woodworker from Nazareth, whose preaching at the beginning (only a few months previously) was only a call to conversion in view of the coming of the Kingdom of God?

This affirmation of his own importance is much more the case with John, where we continually hear similar tones, often with accent on the "I". In the Greek original and also in the Latin translation this accentuation comes to light through the use of the emphatic *ego*. This accentuation betrays as a rule an implicit contrast, mostly to Israel and its leaders, the Jewish priestly caste, as is the case in: *I am* the good, i.e. the genuine, the ideal shepherd, *I am* the door for the sheep, *I am* the true vine, and no longer the disappointing Israel. When the Samaritan woman says to him at Jacob's well that she knows the Messiah is coming, his reaction is: "*I am* that Messiah", whereas in the synoptics, as in Matthew 16:20, he explicitly forbids his disciples to call him by this name.

The fact that Jesus' language in John's gospel is so different from that in the synoptics, which on average are far more historically reliable, makes the authenticity of these *I*-am-words all the more suspect. Jesus cannot have spoken like this. Here Jesus himself is not the one speaking. It is the evangelist who is making Jesus his mouthpiece. However, in Joseph Ratzinger's book on Jesus no doubt is expressed about the historical reliability of Jesus' words. Ratzinger explains the difference from the synoptics with the difference between the listeners. What Jesus says in the synoptics was, according to Ratzinger, meant for everyone in general; what he says in John's gospel was meant for an inner circle, to which also John the Apostle belonged. The evangelist whom we call John, is for Ratzinger the Apostle himself or at the very least one of his disciples, who faithfully preserved his teacher's words for posterity. But today hardly any biblical scholar still accepts the identification of the evangelist with the Apostle.

It would therefore be very strange if John had put only the *I-am* words into Jesus' mouth. At any rate, in a whole series of texts it is clear Jesus is not the one speaking, but the evangelist himself. This is true, for example, of Jesus' conversation at night with Nicodemus in chapter 3. No one was there. Who could have handed down the content and the actual words? The same applies to Jesus' conversation with the Samaritan woman from Sichar at Jacob's well in chapter 4. The author says explicitly in v.8, immediately after the arrival of the woman, that the disciples had gone into the village to buy food. Thus there were no witnesses to this conversation, which means that the author must have thought up the conversation himself. The long speech of Jesus after the Last Supper is another example. About 70 years later, the author, who was not present, manages to repeat what Jesus for the length of four chapters is supposed to have said in farewell. The conclusion to be drawn is clear: here, too, the evangelist has Jesus speak in the way a dramatic poet presents his characters and has them say what he wants them to say. We cannot maintain with any certainty that any of the many words spoken by Jesus in the fourth gospel really come from him. We can even dare to say with some certainty that not one single word attributed to him by John was really spoken by him.

Such a statement does not, however, need to be a source of annoyance. The words of Jesus in the fourth gospel still point the way, still offer orientation; but they cannot be seen as his authentic words, especially when, on the basis of a mythological tradition, one believes that Jesus is God in human form. All of these words would in this case be infallible and absolutely binding on us. That is certainly the way they have been seen in the Church. The words of an evangelist, who was only a believer like ourselves, have become the basis for dogmatic statements, used in theological debates to prove a particular point of view. That which was meant to inspire and enlighten thus became a source of wrangling within the Church, as the first four Councils have shown.

Therefore, what has been said above about the miracle stories in John's gospel, namely, that they were thought up by the evangelist, applies also to the words of Jesus in his gospel. It certainly applies to the *I-am* words. But what can we do with these apparent words of Jesus which, in fact, are the words of John, who is otherwise unknown to us? They remain exceedingly important, because they are confessions of faith expressed by the Church at the beginning of the second century. With the *I-am* words, the Church confesses, through images of life, light, renewal, resurrection, fruitfulness and joy, the enrichment which active faith in Jesus means for the life of a Christian. Without any difficulty we can make these confessions of faith our own, even today. We only need to change the *I-am* words from the first person into the second and read them as: *You are* the light, the way, the truth, our real shepherd, the vine whose branches we are. For the members of the community of Christian believers, Jesus is all of that. This confession is based on the shared experience of many generations: the experience of the resurrection of Jesus. But this event, crucial for our faith, will only be discussed in detail in Chapter 6.

Review of Jesus' Activity

We know about the life of Jesus only what the gospels tell us: namely, a series of stories, presented as facts, about his activities in the period between his baptism in the Jordan and his early death. We are certain that some of these stories are not invented. The first of these is that he had himself been baptized by John. The evangelists cannot have invented this, because it caused problems for them. Indeed, the baptism by John was understood as the baptism of conversion, and the idea that Jesus was in need of any conversion was inconceivable for the early Church. Further-more, in baptizing Jesus John automatically appeared as the superior figure, and for the early Church Jesus was unquestionably the greater of the two. Therefore Matthew (3:14-15) attempts to reverse the historical positions of Jesus and John with regard to this baptism. In Luke's gospel it is even no longer said explicitly that Jesus had himself been baptized by John, and in the fourth gospel there is no longer any mention of the baptism of Jesus at all. Naturally, the wonderful events: that the heavens open (how are we to picture this?), and the voice and the dove belong to the language of mythological imagery through which the early Church expressed its belief in the special relationship of Jesus to God.

It is also a fact that Jesus moved around the country as an itinerant preacher and that the main theme of his preaching was the coming of the Kingdom of God, but of a God who was full of love for man. It is also historical that he came into conflict with the Jewish authorities, that he liked to speak in parables, that he befriended the marginalized, that his human greatness and depth were unique. But there are doubts. This applies, above all to his activity as a faith healer who possesses magic powers and heals the sick as if on an assembly line. Or where he drives out devils galore. It applies even more to the nature miracles. Here it is as if he takes on the guise of a magician. How is the modern believer to react to this?

In contrast to the traditional Church's stance he will no longer read these stories as reliable reports but as inventions. Not necessarily thought out by the evangelists themselves, although with John this could be the case. With the three others the stories are likely to have their origin in oral tradition. Probably the evangelists themselves believed the historical reality of the events they narrated. In their pre-modern-world faith they believed that God made the impossible possible. That was especially true of the nature miracles. But they did not tell these stories because of their supernatural character. They wanted to announce through these images that he was much more than an itinerant preacher who was calling for conversion, much more than a new John the Baptist, that in his presence and activity the transcendental presence of God could be seen to be at work; The fourth evangelist put it in a nutshell: "He that seeth me, seeth the

Father" (14:9). Not that Jesus was a bodily manifestation of Yahweh, but a human likeness of God.

The intention of the evangelists could also have been to show that Jesus, despite his catastrophic end, was indeed the Messiah the Jews were waiting for. This Messiah would, they hoped, put an end to the plagues under which Israel had suffered since time immemorial. Amongst these plagues were sickness and death. According to the text of the biblical story of creation, God had more hopeful plans for humanity and especially for his people. By establishing the Kingdom of God on earth, the Messiah would restore God's creation which had come apart at the seams. The evangelists preached that in the person of Jesus the Messiah had in fact come. They did this by showing him as a mighty exorcist and miraculous healer. Seen in this light, those mythological stories are nothing more than avowals of the early Church that Jesus was God's Messiah, long-awaited by the Jews.

If we read the miracle stories as symbolical language, the rational perspectives of modernity can have no further issues with them. Symbols are not subject to the critique of pure reason. Only what is meant by them. And here these symbols emphasize the human transcendence of Jesus. It is true that only John explicitly treats his miracle stories as symbols by calling them "signs". Signs always point to something else. And as the saying goes: we should not look at the finger that points, but at that to which it points.

With the synoptics, on the other hand, we often have the impression that with the miracle stories they are relating pure facts. Jesus is presented as a miraculous healer and thereby as a mythical being. But perhaps there is sometimes another intention expressed, for example, in the words: "Thy faith hath made thee whole." Possibly the synoptics, too, are thinking of another kind of healing, of which the story is only giving an image. This applies also to the nature miracles, where Old Testament stories can be seen in the background suggesting a spiritual interpretation. No matter what, we must in any case read the miracle stories, even those of the synoptics, as symbolic stories with a catechetic aim. Only in this way can the modern believer see Jesus of Nazareth emerge from the fog of mythology, as a person like ourselves, but one who was much greater and deeper than we are, much more like God.

The Words of Jesus in the Synoptic Gospels

We must therefore free ourselves of the illusion that in the symbolically intended stories of the synoptics we are seeing the historical Jesus at work. But these stories form only a small minority of the texts in the synoptic gospels. These texts consist for the most part of words of Jesus which relate to everyday life, for example his so-called Sermon on the Mount, which is not a sermon but a collection of varied sayings of Jesus. The same is true of his parables or of his discussions with the Scribes and Pharisees. Naturally, he is always speaking from within his own pre-modern world, and that means: never without some mythological colouring. The mental framework in which he and also the biblical authors lived, was pre-scientific. But to see God at work in all things and to give witness to it as Jesus did, does not necessarily amount to doing injustice to everyday reality.

But we should also rid ourselves of another illusion, namely, that in the gospels we are hearing Jesus' very own words. We are hearing only the words of the author, and he has drawn them from the oral tradition. Furthermore, even the oral tradition has not recorded Jesus' very own words. For, to begin with, Jesus spoke Aramaic. Those who heard him, repeated in Aramaic what they had heard, but certainly not without slight changes and adaptations. People are not recording devices. Their listeners faithfully, but again and again with slight changes, passed on the content of what they had heard, which was then afterwards translated into Greek. In the gospels, with the exception of a few Aramaic expressions, we have only the Greek translation of what Jesus is supposed to have said. But translation always means interpretation and adaptation, and in this process the translator's own ideas and representations always play a role. If ten people translate the same sentence, the result is ten slightly varied versions. Thus the Greek translation reproduces the words of Jesus only in an approximation of their original meaning.

That brings us to the question about the exact meaning and application of his words. For example, of whom is he speaking when he speaks of the Son of Man? Of himself, as the Messiah from the house of David or of the heavenly Son of Man in Daniel 7:13? And what does the Kingdom of God mean concretely for him? Does he understand it in an intramundane sense or even politically? And how does it come about? Or whom does he mean, when in Matthew 25 he speaks of the final judgement by the King, appearing in glory? What he says about this is confusing. Sometimes his statements are even contradictory. For instance, he says on one occasion that he is there only for the Jewish people (15:24), and therefore not for the heathens, and that his disciples should have nothing to do with heathens (Matthew 10:6). But on another occasion he says that they should take their message to all peoples (Luke 24:47). Sometimes his statements cannot be accepted because they are extremely exaggerated (Mark 11:23) or because they contradict our daily experience (Matthew 18:19). Again there are others which it is simply not possible to carry out (Matthew 5:29) or which make it impossible to belong any further to his disciples (Luke 14:33) – and it would be easy to add to this list of examples.

There is no problem in assuming that Jesus said such things and that he even consciously exaggerated their formulation in order to challenge any superficial and seemingly natural way of thinking and to arrive at a deeper insight. In any case we should not take these statements literally, but ask ourselves each time what they are calling on us to do. The problem is that only he knows, and that we cannot ask him, so that we have to work out with one another the most plausible answer and assume that this answer is not much more than a cautious guess at what Jesus could have meant. Did he consider a rule to be binding for everyone or only for a particular group like the apostles, or to be binding in all cases or just in the concrete case which confronted him? Was his call to be understood as a fundamental demand or only as an ideal to strive after? Are we really meant to swear no more oaths (Mark 5:34) or to hate our parents (Luke 14:26) or not to concern ourselves with the burial of our dead (Luke 9:60)? A currently relevant example is his statement about divorce in Matthew 19:6-9, which unmarried Church leaders made into an absolute law before they then went to all kinds of trouble to find a solution to the resulting problems. Again and again, the words of the itinerant preacher, Jesus of Nazareth, spoken 2,000 years ago, pose questions for us. Naturally the situation is still aggravated, when these problematic words are taken to be the infallible and absolutely binding words of a Godman.

What we read from the words of Jesus is therefore often not what he says to us himself, but what we ourselves think and consider important. Even if we succeeded in exactly reconstructing his authentic words, we would not know any better than before what exactly he meant. Therefore, the trouble the American Jesus Seminar gives itself to determine with 100% certainty what statements are his, or with only 70% certainty, or with only 50% or which statements are not his at all, is wasted energy.

In any case, we must keep in mind that the words of Jesus, even his very own, are still human words and not oracular words of a *theos*. Thus we cannot accept them blindly and think that we definitely have to put them into practice, and we cannot impose them on others as commandments. If they don't appear realistic to us, we must at least try to find out what basic conviction of Jesus is expressed in them. We can then work out what is the corresponding attitude and action for us today.

The differences and contradictions between the evangelists need not astonish or ruffle us. What we read in the gospels is not a printout from a dictaphone. Jesus' words have gone first through the filter of the anonymous oral tradition, then through the filter of the translator, and finally through the filter of the evangelist. Each of these three filters has left its imprint on the final result. Otherwise, how could we explain that Matthew and Luke hand down different formulations of the Our Father or of the Beatitudes or of the words spoken by Jesus over the chalice at the Last Supper? These differences teach us that we only have approximate knowledge of what Jesus actually said. Some of his statements – if they are, in fact, his, which is not always certain – remain, despite all attempts to interpret them, obscure or puzzling or confusing and contradictory.

But even the approximate knowledge we have of what he said, is enough for us to see the path he is pointing out to us: namely, do not judge, be merciful because God also is merciful, do not discriminate, do not gather riches, do not retaliate, treat other people the way you would like to be treated yourself, work for the coming of the Kingdom of God on earth, blessed is he who is not violent, give to those who beg, do good to those who are bad to you, be prepared to sacrifice your life for the cause of justice. Fundamentally he preaches a selfless attitude, which is diametrically opposed to our tendency to seek our own advantage at the expense of others. This attitude was his own fundamental attitude, and it proceeded from his total union with the Unlimited Love which he called God or Father. And he acted himself entirely in this spirit. It is inconceivable that he would not have taken his Sermon on the Mount seriously himself. For him the reign of God, which he, along with the whole of Israel, was looking out for, amounted to the reign of love. His Sermon on the Mount gave concrete shape to this reign and brought it about that rules and laws were no longer of prime importance. The one great law, to which all other laws were subordinate, was in his eyes the law of charity. He had come to the unshakeable conviction that the essence of God is love and he was so full of this certainty that he was ready to give up everything for the proclamation of this image of God, even his life. His death was the consequence of this preaching. For history teaches us that people who think their own image of God is threatened by another one, often resort to murder to remove this threat. Where God is concerned, it is all or nothing. That explains for example, the merciless crushing by the Inquisition of the Albigenses or Waldenses or Lutherans, or the almost continuous and often murderous persecution of Jews in Christian society. Likewise, many Jews in leading circles saw in Jesus' different view of God a dangerous threat to the sacred values of the Jewish tradition, and they made sure, with the help of the Prefect Pontius Pilate, that his voice would be silenced. Chapter 5 deals with this matter.

CHAPTER FIVE

Crucified under Pontius Pilate, Died and was Buried

The creed immediately made of the historical Jesus of Nazareth a mythological being. He was "conceived of the Holy Spirit", or more accurately "of holy Spirit" as it is expressed in the oldest Greek confessions of faith. In the gospels, which are the basis of confessions of faith, the Spirit does not yet appear as a person. It is, as in the Old Testament, simply Yahweh's creative life-giving breath. Anyone who lives is breathing. The same applies also to the living God. Therefore according to the creed, Jesus is the result of God's creative breathing and not the result of sexual intercourse, although this contradicts all laws of human physiology. The next phrase: "born of the virgin Mary" is a superfluous repetition of the same idea. What kind of "good tidings" this confession of faith, in the obscure language of myth, brings to the modern believer can be seen in chapter 3.

But then the creed suddenly seems to make way for a sober historical communication: "(he) suffered under Pontius Pilate, (was) crucified, died and (was) buried." Unfortunately, in this way the creed misses the whole point of the life of Jesus. If we focus only on his birth and his death, it is as if his life and words were unimportant. That would be a crass mistake. The famous marble pulpits of Nicola and of Giovanni Pisano in the cathedrals of Pisa, Pistoia and Siena show how widespread this error had become in the Middle Ages: on the 6 or 8 panels of those pulpits there is no trace of the public life of Jesus. All the more space is taken up by the legendary scenes of his birth and, along with them, by his death on the cross. But if Jesus is important for us, it is above all on the basis of what he said and did in his public life, from his baptism in the Jordan River until his early death on the cross, which was only a frightful consequence of his public activity.

Behind this impoverishment is lurking the teaching of redemption thought up by Paul, in which the most crucial event is the cruel death of Jesus. The problem for Paul was that on the one hand he believed that Jesus was the Messiah, yet on the other hand the Messiah could not suffer a wretched death, as Jesus had suffered. He had to be victorious. Paul escaped from this dilemma by interpreting Jesus' death on the cross as a sacrifice of expiation, a cultic category with which, as a Jewish Scribe, he was very familiar. In the book of Leviticus, three whole chapters (5 to 7) are devoted to the regulations to be observed in such sacrifices of expiation. And so in the letters of Paul the life, words and deeds of Jesus have hardly any role to play, not even when, in the Letter to the Philippians (2:5), he uses the humble attitude of Jesus as a model for the attitude of the believers. He does not illustrate this humble attitude with the deeds and words of Jesus in his public life, but only with his *kenosis* as a pre-existent heavenly being who becomes man and shows he is ready to take on death on the cross – which God is supposed to require of him to redeem the sins of the world. There too, as he mostly does, Paul is exclusively concerned with the violent death of Jesus and his spilt blood. This blood is the alpha and omega of Paul's doctrine of salvation, for with his blood the guilt of Adam is paid for and through his blood we are justified (Romans 5:9). In the pious language of ecclesiastical texts and songs we then hear that Jesus through his holy cross has saved the world and opened again the gates of Heaven, closed because of our sins. One could ask what Paul's argument would have been if Jesus had not been crucified but had been killed without bloodshed, as for example through drowning or hanging.

We have sucked in Paul's notion of redemption with our mother's milk and confessed it without questioning it. But this notion is saturated with mythology and for modernity it is completely out of date and incomprehensible. It presupposes an anthropomorphic, law-giving God in a supernatural world, in which the same kind of justice prevails as in this sublunary world. In this system of justice every misdeed demands punishment. If anyone through criminal behaviour has burdened himself with guilt, this guilt has to be paid for, restoration must be made and the crime expiated. Justice in Heaven (thought of as corresponding to the human model) works the same way. Therefore "sin", by which transgression of a divine law is meant, must be punished. But according to Pauline theology Jesus has taken this punishment on himself, representing all of us. He has consequently become a kind of scapegoat, taking away the guilt of others. He atones for our guilt with his life, wipes away our debt with his blood. According to Paul we are thereby redeemed, i.e. saved from the punishment we deserve.

Farewell to Expiation and Reconciliation

For a modern believer that is a completely unreal way of speaking, for that whole juridical process takes place outside of each individual's existence and does not touch or change his deeper being. If my guilt is forgiven, which means that I avoid the punishment incurred, I still remain exactly what I was before, just as far removed from God as I was.

Paul's idea of reconciliation through a sacrifice of expiation is a category which no longer means anything to us. Firstly, reconciliation presupposes that there had been a quarrel between God and us, something totally human which we cannot apply to God. Secondly, an expiatory sacrifice only has meaning if one has to deal with an irate Sovereign, whose mercy can be bought with presents, preferably involving blood. Does Paul really think that God is pleased if, in honour of Him, we deprive ourselves of something we would like to have kept? That is exactly what sacrifice is! Or that He will be pleased and inclined to mercy, if the blood of an innocent animal or even of an innocent person, like the blood of Jesus of Nazareth, is spilt? Expiatory sacrifice is a purely mythological construct which makes of the God of love a cold ruler, who can be bribed.

But if God is the love that produces everything, the situation is quite different. In this case sin is the refusal to be led by love and therefore by God. And the right response to this guilty refusal is no longer punishment and penance but conversion. In the parable of the lost son there is no mention of punishment and penance. The only thing God wants, as Jesus teaches us in this amazing parable, is clearly that we change our ways. As soon as the guilty son does exactly that, all problems are over. But no one can bring about my inner conversion without me. That conversion is an existential process in me. Representatives and scapegoats can achieve nothing in this. Only God as Fundamental Love can move me to this conversion by opening my eyes to my foolishness, attracting me and awakening in me a loving disposition. This is exactly what He does through Jesus, in whose activity and words He expresses Himself and makes Himself visible. And He does this through the love of mankind which Jesus manifests in freely accepting his death on the cross.

Jesus simply gives an example of love, and because God has breathed into us a longing to live and therefore to love, we know by looking at Jesus that it is exactly that which our heart needs. Thus the readiness to follow him is awakened in us. By our turning to him and making his way ours, the saving conversion is accomplished in us. The stronger our belief in him, i.e. the more resolute our turning to him, the more we are inwardly healed. In the language of the Church one then speaks of "being saved". Saved from what? Not from condemnation and punishment, but from the power of self-love, which is continually threatening to lead us astray from the path of love of our fellow men. Thus it is not as a child in the manger that Jesus saves us, but as the prophet filled with God's love, whom we know from his brief appearance in human history.

Back to the Creed

Let us return to the creed, in the form of the Symbol of the Apostles, which after "died and was buried" continues with "descended into hell", translating in this manner the Latin *descendit ad inferos*. This little phrase is missing in the great Latin creed, which is the translation of the Greek profession of faith of Nicaea-Constantinople. It appears for the first time in a Latin creed from the year 404. Its meaning is not clear. Is it merely a powerful repetition of "dead and buried", as modern translations suggest? Or does it mean a mythical descent of Jesus into the underworld? The latter interpretation can find support in the First Epistle of Peter, where we read in 3:19 that after his death Jesus "went in spirit and preached for the spirits in prison". A more accurate translation from the Latin *descendit ad inferos* would in fact be: he descended into the realm of the dead, thus into the mythical underworld of antiquity. Although the text is not in the Greek creeds, under the influence of Peter's letter the notion of a real descent has played an important role precisely in the Orthodox world. This descent is visually represented countless times in Greek and Russian icons as a symbol of Jesus' victory over death and devil. But if with modernity, we have once and for all left behind that notion of a mythical underworld, one can be glad to encounter in the modern translations of the Symbol of the Apostles instead of this crass mythology a somewhat incorrect but no longer mythological translation.

But the seemingly historical intermezzo about the death and burial of Jesus is, on closer inspection, not at all meant as an historical statement. The creed is not interested in the historical as such. It simply sums up what the gospel says. And the evangelists did not intend to report historical facts, but to show history in the light of faith. The mention of Jesus' death on the cross has therefore a different function from that of the reports of Flavius Josephus or Cornelius Tacitus. What the evangelists say about the death of Jesus is not simply communicated, but rather interpreted. The phrase in the creed about the crucifixion and death of Jesus should be read as a concessive phrase, which prepares a powerful contrast to what follows: crucified and died, yes, but risen on the third day!

Before continuing now with the Passion, first another important comment. In contrast to the public life of Jesus the narration of his death is almost completely free of mythology. Only a few minor details are mythological. In Luke's gospel an angel appears to fortify Jesus on the Mount of Olives (22:43), and Jesus heals an ear that has been hacked off; in each of the synoptics, at the moment of his death the veil of the temple is rent from top to bottom and in the afternoon there is darkness for three hours. Finally, (only in Matthew) the earth shakes when Jesus dies, the rocks are split, the graves open and some just people who have died are awakened from the dead and appear to many in Jerusalem. There are no other purely mythological elements in the synoptics. In the presentation of the last hours of Jesus in John's gospel there are none at all. Only in the prelude to the events does a voice come from above (12:28); and talk of Satan is connected with Judas (13:2).

Mythology always requires interpretation. The fact that at the death of Jesus the temple veil protecting the Holy of Holies was rent from top to bottom is a sign that the time of the temple and its cult is past. Previously the High Priest was the only one who could go behind the curtain and approach God, and that, only once in the year, on the Day of Atonement. Now the hour has come (for Jesus "the hour" is a word which refers to his death and glorification) that everyone can approach God and adore him in spirit and truth (John 4:23). Both the darkness in the broad daylight and the earthquake and its effects are reminiscent of the catastrophes which, according to the prophets, will accompany the day on which Yahweh will sit in judgement. In Matthew's gospel (24:29-30) they accompany the coming of the victorious Son of Man. The death of Jesus *is* therefore his coming in glory. And he is the Son of Man seen by Daniel. The resurrection of the dead will then take place, according to the Book of Daniel (12:2). That it happens already with the death of Jesus shows that this death is at the same time the triumph of the Son of Man.

Naturally, mythological thinking is also at work where the four evangelists announce the fulfilment of Old Testament statements, which they first had to see as prophecies, even though they are not that at all. Matthew sees this fulfilment in the purchase of the potter's field (27:9-10) after Judas has thrown his 30 pieces of silver into the temple; Mark (15:28) and Luke (12:37) see it when Jesus is to be crucified with two criminals; John sees it as early as Jesus' entry into Jerusalem riding on an ass (12:14-15), and then, when he speaks about the lack of faith of Jesus' listeners (12:38-41), about the betrayal by Judas (13:18), about the casting of lots for Jesus' garments (19:24), about Jesus' thirst (19:28), and finally about the decision of the soldiers not to break his legs but to pierce his side (19:36-37). In chapter three it has already been explained why the idea of fulfilling the Scriptures presupposes mythological thinking.

Judaism is rightly incensed by the notion that the right access to their own Holy Scripture should depend on Christian interpretations. The biblical message was meant not for Christians but for the Jews, who, as the primary addressees, are best placed to know how to interpret it. The Torah does in no way prophesy what Christians take from it as divine prophecies. Judaism resents the Christian interpretation of its texts as sheer presumption – coming from a group which had begun as a Jewish sect, but then separated from the Jewish community and had thereby forfeited its Jewish rights. One of these was the right to interpret the biblical message in an authoritative way. In what follows it will be shown that precisely this reference back to the Old Testament gives an answer to the question where tradition and/or the evangelists derive their knowledge about the end of Jesus' life.

The Non-Historical Character of John's Passion

The other limit of the historical – the creative fantasy – played a much greater part in the four Passion stories than we are inclined to think. Unconsciously we read the story of Jesus' last hours as reported fact, as if a journalist had been there, accurately writing down everything for us. That is a crass mistake.

This is most clearly the case with John's gospel. Above, it has been shown in detail that this gospel is essentially a profound but often enough mythological meditation about Jesus. Historical aims are foreign to John. As he says himself, with his book he wants to bring his readers to believe in Jesus as God's Messiah, so that through this faith they might have life (20:31). But what is true of the chapters about the public life of Jesus, is true also of the two chapters (18 and 19) which John has devoted to the suffering and death of Jesus.

A comparison of John with the synoptics, which are historically more reliable, reveals a whole series of differences and even contradictions. Thus it becomes clear that we cannot rely on John's account. We should therefore always ask ourselves what the hidden intention of his unhistorical version might be. In John's gospel Jesus does not suffer agony in the Garden of Olives; he is not kissed by Judas; with his answer "I am (the one you seek)" he makes such a strong impression on the armed troop of soldiers that they recoil in shock and collapse on the ground, as if in this answer they heard an echo of the divine name with which Yahweh made himself known to Moses. Also in John's gospel, Jesus is questioned by Annas, not by the High Priest Caiaphas, and in the praetorium he holds two historically impossible conversations with Pilate (18:33-38 and 19:9-11). Pilate spoke no Aramaic and Jesus probably no Greek, to say nothing of Latin, and in the room there was no secretary taking notes who could have passed on the content of those conversations to John or his informant. Besides, the synoptics say expressly that Jesus, to Pilate's great surprise, remained silent in Pilate's presence (Mark 15:5, Matthew 27:14). It follows that John thought up these conversations himself. In this way he wanted to underline the true nature of the Messianic Kingdom of Jesus. Striking in John's account is the increasingly stronger emphasis on this Kingdom, the greater Jesus' humiliation. John is also the only one who mentions the breaking of legs and the piercing with a lance, both in order to draw attention to the fulfilment of Old Testament words. He is also the only one who says that the mother of Jesus (that she is called Mary is never mentioned in his whole gospel) stood by the cross. Clearly the synoptics know nothing about her presence. They do know of some women, amongst them Mary Magdalen, who stood looking from a distance. From a distance, because at an execution no relatives and friends of the crucified were, in any circumstances, allowed to be near.

Nevertheless, according to John the mother of Jesus stands by the cross, and with her, along with a few other women, also the mysterious "disciple whom Jesus loved" (19:26) and of whose existence the synoptics know absolutely nothing. This disciple appears for the first time at the Last Supper, therefore right at the end of his gospel. All attempts of bible critics to identify him with a real disciple of Jesus have failed. In the uncritical commentaries on John's gospel it is still often said that this beloved disciple is John, the son of Zebedee. But we may forget that, although this John is always represented as standing with Mary at the cross. It is very probable that with the presence of these two persons the fourth evangelist does not intend to communicate facts, but, as he often does, to paint a symbolic scene. The American exegete John Shelby Spong interprets this scene in a convincing way. That mysterious disciple represents the community of believers, which consists of Jewish Christians. Therefore the woman too (this is also how Jesus addresses her there) is a symbolic figure. She is no longer the physical mother of Jesus, Mary, but a symbol of the Jewish people from which Jesus has been born and with him the Jewish Christian community. The Jewish people, the mother, has problems with this community, which slowly withdraws from her, and she is considering banning them as apostates. The Christian community, for its part, finds it difficult, because of these tensions, to acknowledge that it belongs to this mother. The dying Jesus, who for John is also the Jesus that rises from the dead, calls on mother and son to accept one another. The Christian tradition has given material shape to these symbolic figures, just as it has done with other symbolic figures from John's gospel: Nicodemus, the Samaritan woman, the man born blind, Lazarus. But materializing a symbol and trying to insert it into history, inevitably leads to conflicts and inconsistencies. In the case of the man born blind, and especially in the case of Lazarus, we are confronted with such conflicts head on, and this false impression of historicity meets with no understanding in the modern era.

Questions regarding the Passion story in the synoptic Gospels

But also what the synoptics write about the end of Jesus' life throws up many questions. This applies firstly to the narration of his agony in the Garden of Olives. It is stressed three times that the three disciples were asleep. And Jesus was a stone's throw away from them – so, about 30 metres. Even if they had been wide awake, they would scarcely have been able to hear Jesus' pleading prayer. Still, the evangelists communicate to us its exact content. Also the three disciples certainly did not see the angel who came to strengthen him, and the blood that he sweated (both only in Luke's gospel). When Jesus is captured, they all flee. Where to? Surely not to Jerusalem, into the lion's den. For according to John 20:19 they were very afraid of "the Jews" although they were Jews themselves. Therefore all that is said in Luke's gospel about their presence in Jerusalem on the day of Easter, as the two disciples returned from Emmaus (Luke 24:33), and about the race to the sepulchre on Easter morning between Peter and the "disciple whom Jesus loved" (John 20:3) must have been invented.

But if none of them had remained in Jerusalem, they would not have witnessed the events on Good Friday. What, then, was the source of the precise reports about the different steps in the Passion story? Peter can have known something. He had turned back and had from a safe distance followed the soldiers with their prisoner Jesus. All four evangelists concur in saying that he ventured in as far as the courtyard of the High Priest. But even there he could not have known anything about what happened inside the palace. So what is the source of Mark's precise information about an interrogation which, according to Jewish law, could not have taken place because it was night time, whereas the courts could only have a legally valid sitting in daytime? Or how did Matthew find out the content of the message which Pilate's wife sent to her husband? Also nothing is known historically about a customary right of the Jewish people to demand amnesty for a condemned person, even though the evangelists maintain that such a right existed. The scene of the crowning with thorns is undoubtedly conceivable, but it is much less likely that one of the soldiers would afterwards have told Jesus' followers, with plenty of details, how lustily they had mocked him in the Antonia Fortress. And probably the same applies to the confrontation with Herod Antipas.

The Passion story is related by the evangelists half a century after the events in such a way that all seems logical and evident, so that one does not even ask how they could know all of this so well. And there is no satisfactory answer to that question. At any rate, the synoptics used what was related in the oral tradition, but without asking from which source this tradition had drawn its information. Luke does say in the introduction to his gospel that he has carefully examined everything that was handed down from eye-witnesses, and yet he supplies information which normally none of Jesus' circle at that time could have had. The answer that followers of Jesus, using creative imagination, made up stories from rumours and surmises, can provoke protest. But what medieval piety did unquestioningly is surely not inconceivable in that first half century as well. The creators of the Stations of the Cross have thought up an encounter of Jesus with his mother on the way to Golgotha and a Veronica that wiped the face of Jesus and the three-fold fall of Jesus under the cross (and what about Simon of Cyrene?) and the image of the Pietà with her dead son on her lap. One can also think of the detailed description of Jesus' sufferings, which visionaries like Catherine Emmerich have given us.

This process of development and accretion in the course of time is also found in the so-called seven last words of Jesus on the cross, of which very probably not a single one is authentic, because none of the venerators of Jesus, man or woman, stood near enough to the cross to hear them. Mark knows only one sole word of Jesus on the cross, namely, the initial verse of the 22nd Psalm. The same applies to Matthew, who for the most part follows him accurately. Some years later Luke does not know precisely this one word, but he knows three others: a plea for forgiveness for his executioners (23:34), a promise that the "good thief" will be in paradise that same day (23:43), and the trusting verse 6 of Psalm 31, which Jesus prays as he dies (23:46). These words are therefore invented by Luke or his source. Some years later again, John also knows three words of Jesus on the cross, but this time different ones: “See, thy son” and “See, thy mother”, “I am thirsty” (19:28) and the almost triumphant “It is accomplished” (19:30).

The Old Testament Source

We have learnt to read the Passion story as a report of historical events. A series of Old Testament texts seems to justify this. They show such striking agreement with this report that they can be cited as gripping illustrative material of it and thus seem to confirm the truth of the gospel narratives. This applies above all to two relatively long texts: Psalm 22 and the Song of the suffering Servant of Yahweh in Isaiah 53. The Passion gives the impression, because of the noticeable congruities with these texts, which then are understood as prophecies, that it is their fulfilment. But the Psalmist and the Second Isaiah have in no way prophesied events which were to happen 500 years later. They have simply described, on the basis of their belief in God and reflecting on their own experiences, what the just man can suffer, but expressed also their certainty that God does not abandon him to his bitter fate, but, true to his word, saves him from all harm.

Therefore in reading the Passion we must reverse our perspective. We should not begin with the cleverly composed story of the evangelists, but with the Old Testament texts, for these are the quarry from which the narrators have taken the material for their story of the last hours in Jesus’ life. How far their story corresponds to the facts is a very difficult question to answer. Perhaps even Mark himself (or his source) for lack of reliable eye-witnesses has simply used Psalm 22 and the Song of the suffering Servant of Yahweh, along with other texts from the Old Testament, to flesh out his story of the Passion. Those Old Testament texts seemed indeed to contain really accurate predictions about much that Jesus would experience and did, in fact, experience, along with the joyful message that he would finally be victorious. Moreover, together with the material of the stories they also supplied interpretations. For example, we can read from Isaiah 53 that, in his suffering, the Servant of Yahweh is representing others, wiping out the guilt of his fellow men. Such an interpretation would give the suffering and death of Jesus, which would otherwise seem meaningless, a rich signifycance. In his narration Mark presented those prophetic texts as having become reality in Jesus and thus as "fulfilled". Luke later took over Matthew's narration and enriched it with some new elements: with the suicide of Judas, with the hand-washing of Pilate, with the intervention of Pilate's wife and with the mocking of Jesus in the palace of Herod Antipas. John, for his part, developed on this foundation his own mystical/-theological perspective on the meaning of the suffering and death of Jesus.

In all of this we should not lose sight of the following. The only written source we have about the end of Jesus' life before Mark published his Passion shortly after the year 70, is Paul. But what Paul knew about the end of Jesus' life seems to be limited to the capture of Jesus and his death on the cross. In his conversations with Cephas-Petrus in the two weeks he spent with him (Galatians 1:18) he apparently heard little more about Jesus' last hours. Or perhaps this was simply of no particular interest to him. In any case, in his seven authentic letters there is no reference to Jesus' Passion. Paul's only contribution is to interpret the death of Jesus as a sacrifice of expiation. But with this interpretation he tells us nothing at all about Jesus' last hours, about which, however, ten years later Mark is able to deliver a continuous narration.

The Burial of Jesus

The critical question about the reliability of what Mark, and in his wake the others, report about the end of Jesus' life, should be seen also in connection with the epilogue to Mark's Passion, the burial of Jesus. Anyone who looks carefully at what should have happened between the death of Jesus at the ninth hour (Mark 15:33) – namely, between three o'clock in the afternoon and the beginning of the Sabbath rest three hours later – can only shake his head in disbelief. "It was already evening", Mark's account begins. Thus the ninth hour had already begun, and there was little time left before the beginning of the Sabbath. Can all that Mark relates, really have happened in the couple of hours before sunset: Joseph of Arimathea going up to the Fortress Antonia, the audience with Pilate, the confirmation by the officer that Jesus was dead, Joseph's return to the city, his purchase of the linen cloth, the fetching of the necessary tools and helpers, the walk with these to Golgotha which was outside the city, the time needed to remove the body that was nailed to the cross, and the ritual of burial? Could all of that really have happened in the time between late afternoon and sunset?

Finally, there is yet another question: who took down the two who were crucified with Jesus and what was done with their corpses? John writes that the soldiers had been commanded to break their legs and to take them down. The dead could not, in Jewish law, which was also approved by the Romans, be left hanging on the cross during the Sabbath. The soldiers thus carried out this order (19:32). And what will they have done with the corpses – and perhaps that of Jesus as well? It is quite conceivable that they hurriedly put them into a quickly dug mass grave. That was the norm with collective executions. John's story about Joseph of Arimathea, which he must have known from the synoptics, begins only afterwards, as does the equally improbable report about Nicodemus with his hundred pounds of aloe. All very confusing and contradictory. In the analysis of the stories of apparitions some of this will have to come into play again.

In Reza Aslan's book, the story of Jesus' life ends with his death. To support his opinion that Jesus was a "zealot", a pious and noble pseudo-Messiah doomed to failure, he can only have recourse to material which can be found in the period of Jesus' life. After the death of Jesus he can only try to track down what people who had known or heard him, saw in him and said about him, and what influence he had exerted in these ways on history. In the title of his book this part is called: The Birth of a Religion. But this second part has no influence on his notion of the person Jesus in the first part, where his view is completely determined by what he has taken from the sources (used, alas, very selectively) about what the living Jesus did and said.

But for believers, both pre-modern and modern, it is different. For them, what happened after Jesus' death – and here the key concept is "resurrection" – plays a decisive role in answering the question about who Jesus of Nazareth really is. This is dealt with in the next chapter.

CHAPTER SIX

Rose from the Dead on the Third Day?

For Paul and his Christians, the death of Jesus on the cross was a *skandalon,* a stumbling block. How could the Messiah and Saviour of Israel sent by God so wretchedly fail? Thus they reacted as Peter reacted in Matthew 16:22 after Jesus at Caesarea Philippi predicted his Passion: "God forbid! Such a thing can never happen to you." Paul then went to a lot of trouble to find a place in his ideas as a believer for this *skandalon of a crucified Messiah.* Fortunately, for him Jesus was only God's Messiah and not God himself who became man and was crucified – as many theologians in blind fidelity to Nicaea still call him.

For modern man, however, the inconceivable and unimaginable is not Jesus' death on the cross. This is understandable and even almost natural, if we think of the contrast between, on the one hand, Jesus' conception of God and his actions which followed from it, and, on the other hand, the religious ideas of the Jewish leaders. It is not unusual for religious differences and tensions to lead to murder. Religion deals with absolutes. The greater the conviction pious people bring to their assertion of the rights of God, the less room is left for compromise. The innumerable burnings at the stake in the course of the history of Christianity show this with brutal clarity. Today this is clear in Islam with the murderous persecution by the Sunnite Islamic State of the Shiites, Yazidi, Christians and all other kinds of infidels, as they call them. In the eyes of the Jewish leaders Jesus blasphemed against Yahweh by representing him in a way which clearly deviated from the official view, and he propagated his erroneous ideas in his preaching. He had to be silenced. They believed that this was what God wanted.

Thus for modern people the execution of Jesus is not inconceivable. Really inconceivable is the affirmation by the Churches that he rose from the dead. This defies all reason. That a dead person could come to life again and emerge from the grave is simply unthinkable. Yet in the Christian world of the past it was easy to believe that and to see death as a long sleep, from which man could wake up, if and when God wanted. But despite the expressions "gone to sleep" or "eternal rest", modern people no longer understand death as a sleep. We get up after sleep, strengthened and renewed. People never awake from death. Physiology tells us why not. As soon as the heart stops it no longer pumps blood, enriched with oxygen, through the brain, and after a very short time of being deprived of oxygen this delicate tissue begins to decay. Of the billions of cerebral junctions which maintain and guide the wonderful processes of a living organism, soon none of them functions any more. Rising from the dead would mean that this unbelievably complex whole – much more complex than a super-calculator with its innumerable microscopic components tuned in to one another – would have without help regenerated itself and have become capable of functioning again. Or a power beyond the cosmos would have intervened with its magic. But for modern people there is no longer any such power. Therefore, anyone who speaks of resurrection is unconsciously still living in a magical and mythical world. The fact that in the modern Western world countless people nevertheless have no problem believing in the resurrection amounts to a collective refusal to see the obvious truth, and is an annoyance and offence to modernity. To confess such a belief clearly makes a mockery of all sound thinking. This seems to create a dilemma for the modern believer. Either he acknowledges with modernity the impossibility of the bodily resurrection of Jesus, and then he ceases to be a believer – for his resurrection is at the heart of the Christian message – or he stays with his pious conviction that Jesus rose from the dead, and he then excludes himself from modernity.

But is there really a dilemma? Is there no third possibility? Yes, there is. We should free the concept of resurrection from its mythological garb and translate the essential aspect that then emerges, in such a way, that it no longer clashes with modern science. The concept of resurrection was born in a pre-modern culture as an attempt, bound up with that culture, to express experiences which in those days could not be formulated differently and better. But in the modern era a different and better formulation is both possible and indispensable.

What were these experiences in those days and still today? Ultimately the liberating experience that we are the object of care of a Fundamental Reality, which produces and sustains all things and is life and is the giver of life. The Jewish-Christian tradition refers to this mysterious Fundamental Reality with the words

Yahweh and God. The way in which this experience is intimately related to the belief in resurrection, will become clear later on. But if the human spirit stems from this wonderful spiritual Fundamental Reality, and is even a finite self-expression of this infinite Mystery, we can expect that every person, if even only implicitly, has some experience of it. Some people are much more sensitive to this experience than others and feel in themselves the impulse to express what they experience. In Israel such highly gifted people were called "prophets", and people recognized in their words something which they experienced themselves to a quite minimal degree. Out of this grew the collective certainty that there existed between this holy Fundamental Reality and the people of Israel a kind of covenant, which to some extent resembled a marriage bond, so that it was possible to speak of election and of Israel as the chosen people. This comparison with a marriage bond is not so strange, because in Jewish marriage, even though it was a genuine partnership arrangement, man and woman were not equal partners. The husband was the lord and master, and this is the way Yahweh was seen in relation to Israel. This image made it clear that loyalty to this covenant would bring life and blessing to Israel, for Yahweh was a God of life and fertility. Creation showed that in a thousand ways.

But the cruel persecution in 170 BC by the Syrian ruler Antiochus Epíphanes (Palestine belonged at that time to the kingdom of Syria), who wanted to put the Jews on the same footing as the other people of his Hellenistic kingdom, showed that loyalty to the covenant could bring, instead of life and blessing, torture and death. That gave Judaism the insight that the life Yahweh promised to them should be given to the victims in another form, for Yahweh remains eternally true to his promises. Here, too, ideas tied to contemporary culture played a decisive role in the concrete representation of how this loyalty would reveal itself. In the Jewish view man was a body infused with spirit, a unity, not a duality made up of a spiritual and therefore immortal soul and a material and therefore mortal body. In the Psalms "my body" means simply "I", just as "my soul" or "my bones" or "my heart" or "my mouth" or "my lips" or "my reins" all mean simply "I", but constantly seen under different aspects. This "I" was equally spiritual and physical and therefore belonging to our world. The life promised to the victims of Antiochus therefore had to be a physical reality within our world. The dead person had to become alive again. And since Judaism didn't practice cremation but only burial, and the dead person lay there as if asleep, the idea was formed that death was something like sleep and that Yahweh would at some time awaken out of this sleep those who had been loyal to Him, and they would rise up, and with this resurrection a new phase of blissful life on earth would begin for them. At the time of Jesus' appearance the idea of resurrection of the just was fairly widespread in Judaism.

That pre-modern idea that the just (originally they alone!) would rise up out of the grave, hence presupposes a series of Jewish, and therefore culturally conditioned, notions and customs. If, with modernity, we have left these behind, we should not only abandon the word "resurrection", but must also give a modern and convincing formulation to the Jewish certainty that the covenant between the God of life and us lasts even beyond death.

But that is more difficult than it seems. The Jewish notions, and especially the language of resurrection that derives from them, have become self-evident through 2000 years of repetition within the Christian tradition. This makes it psychologically difficult to interpret the concept of resurrection differently from the way it has been interpreted since the beginning. Gestalt psychology explains this difficulty using the concept of optical illusion. This concept refers to the possibility of seeing the same phenomenon in two different ways: to see, for instance the drawing of a cube as looked at from above or as looked at from below, but not in both ways at once. If we have seen it the first way, it takes an effort to switch to the second way. Likewise, it takes effort, when we hear the word resurrection, to free ourselves from the traditional and deeply ingrained notion of leaving the grave and focus squarely on the reality to which it really points. Therefore it is desirable to use, instead of that pre-modern word, modern concepts with the same content. It is obvious that if we succeed in finding a new way of thinking about the matter concerned, we'll find also what words are suitable.

To find this new thinking we must give up not only the Jewish concept of man but also the Greek one that has been imprinted in us by that compendium of the Christian doctrine called the catechism. Because Christianity has grown up in the Roman Empire, which was profoundly penetrated by Hellenism, that

Greek notion of man has become that of the Christian doctrine and hence also ours. It holds that man is the combination of a spiritual and therefore immortal soul with a mortal body, which is destined to decay. Obviously the soul is by far the more important of these two parts, and the body is more a burden than a joy. But, looked at more closely, this seemingly obvious concept of man makes the idea of resurrection simply meaningless. For the death of Jesus would then be the liberation of his immortal soul from his mortal body and would mean the entry of his soul into the glory of God. He/it would sit in victory "at the right hand of the Father". Can anything then be lacking to Him/it? Or does one need anything more than union with God? The resurrection of Jesus would therefore only be the return of his already glorified soul into his burdening body. The exuberant rejoicing of the Easter liturgy about the resurrection then becomes incomprehensible. For where is the boundless gain in such a return? Logically we should only rejoice over the death of Jesus, which would be his victorious entry into the glory of God.

In brief, in both the Jewish and the Greek conception the idea of "resurrection", leads into a cul-de-sac. In the Jewish conception the formerly animated organism, once dead, decays completely and, as modern science proves, can no longer be of any use; in the Greek conception the immortal soul that sees God, cannot have the slightest need of a new body. It was first the Enlightenment that opened our eyes to this. Thus in the modern era we have to develop a new concept of man and of resurrection, that is meaningful for a believer.

This new concept is based on the notion that the cosmos, with man as its preliminary high point, is the ever richer developing self-expression of a Fundamental Reality that is spiritual and transcends all the concepts with which human thought tries to grasp things. We can only attempt an approximation to it. The least deficient concepts we can use to speak about that Fundamental Reality seem to be life and love. Here we meet the believers' tradition as it is found in the first epistle of John (4:9) in the formula: "God is love." In this confession the community of believers relies fully on Jesus' experience of the divine. Deep within himself he experienced God as unconditional Love. Hence his spontaneous prayer to Him, addressing him as "Abba": dear Father. Believing in Jesus includes naturally that one tries to share in his relationship to the mysterious God.

The more a person lets himself be led by selfless love, the more he becomes of one essence with God, who is love, and also the more he lives – for God is life. The believer knows Jesus as someone who, driven by the Fundamental Love, has been totally devoted to his fellow men. By sealing this attitude by his death his union with the Fundamental Mystery, God, reached its fullness. That is the modern believer's version of the no longer imaginable reality of what happened to Jesus when he died. It is no longer imaginable, because God is the unimaginable as such. The easily imaginable physical resurrection argues against its truth content.

Something of this modern believer's conception can be found in the mystical vision of John's gospel. In this gospel, Jesus' death on the cross appears as the moment of his glorification or completion. In other words: Jesus experiences his resurrection, when he dies on the cross. The texts in which we find glimpses of this are 12:24 about the grain of wheat that lives fully by dying in the ground; 12:32 about the power that will go out from his death on the cross, so that he will attract all to him; 19:37 the admiring and revering gaze on him just in his apparent defeat. On a more hidden level the fourth evangelist gives us a glimpse of this by emphasizing the regal dignity of Jesus the more he is humiliated. The whole scene with Pilate, which ends with the *Ecce homo* ("Behold the man"), which is not in the synoptics, has essentially this function. For a moment John breaks through the mythological cast of thought of his own pre-modern culture, for which death and resurrection are two distinct steps between which there is a period of sleep in death – in the case of Jesus, 36 hours – and he sees the sacred unity of the two. Then this vision is gone, and his narrative again follows the traditional path.

It now begins to dawn which expressions are suitable, in the language of the modern believer, to replace the expression "resurrection" without any loss of essential content. In pre-modern times "resurrection" served extremely well. It corresponded to the mode of thinking of its time. But in the modern period it has done its duty and can go. In the context of modern thinking, in order to indicate the magnificent event that took place in Jesus' death, we need new formulas that replace advantageously the pre-modern "he has risen". The Scripture itself offers us such formulas, so that the believer does not need to think of the sleep of death and of waking up, in order to celebrate the victory of Jesus. For example: “God has glorified him”, or “has given him the name which is above all names”, or, quite simply: "he lives", or the visual image already mentioned above: “he is sitting at the right hand of the Father”, which points to his becoming one with the unlimited love that is God, or “eternal life” – at least as long as we do not mean by “eternal”: lasting without end but, instead, “life with infinite depth”. Resurrection is therefore only one of the many concepts which the Scripture uses to name the unimaginable event that has happened in Jesus’ death. And precisely this one concept has lost its usefulness for modern-thinking people.

Why give up the ancient notions?

It is undoubtedly much simpler and clearer to stay with the notions which are familiar to us and which are basically ancient Jewish notions: Jesus dies, is buried, remains 36 hours in the grave, as it were, sleeping, wakes up on Sunday morning from this sleep, climbs out of his grave alive and well, with a body that has at its disposal all the qualities and functions it had before his death: he can walk, speak, let people feel him, can make a fire, break bread, eat fried fish – in a word can do everything that every human body can. This is the way the pre-modern Church, which has spontaneously adopted the tradition of the early Church with its Jewish orientation, sees the risen Jesus. This is also the way that, for example, Joseph Ratzinger sees him in his book on Jesus. But Ratzinger obviously does not see the impossibility of bringing back to life a decaying organism, no more than do (apart from a handful of exceptions) the two billion Christians, no matter which confession they belong to. Modern people blink with amazement when they learn this. And they are even more amazed when they hear that this body can, in addition, do what other bodies cannot do: suddenly appear and again disappear, go through closed doors and finally ascend, of itself, from the earth into the sky. Ratzinger believes that he has an answer to this contradiction: the risen Jesus, he writes, “has a real body, but that body is not bound by physical laws.” (II, 291). He is physical, but then again, not physical. In this way we exclude any chance of bringing the message of our faith into modern culture, as if it were meant only for pre-modern culture. The message was indeed very successfully assimilated by pre-modern culture. But all cultures are essentially transitory. Along with pre-modern culture our message would therefore be bound to disappear.

But is it absolutely necessary to relinquish the earlier clear notions and tread the narrow, steep path of a new formulation with notions which are much less clear – merely to keep the door open for modernity? Can we not encounter God even today with the help of the traditional words and forms? Not even one in ten thousand baptized persons in the western world has a problem with the pre-modern notion of a God who intervenes in the cosmos and with a Jesus, who is indeed man, but is at the same time the almighty God, and with the Church's whole mythology and thereby also with the physical resurrection of Jesus on the third day after his death. And in the rest of the world, not one in a million faithful has any problem in believing it. Even the Church leadership apparently has not the slightest problem with these notions. Furthermore, this new formulation will have little effect. Will it prevent the many for whom the pre-modern way of thinking and speaking is a stumbling block, from leaving the Church? Or will it bring back the many who have already left? And what is the basis for thinking that modernity is the world view of the future? In any case it has no counter to the religious expansionist force of Islam, which is in many respects completely pre-modern. What then, after all, is the use of a modern formulation? And wherein lies the usefulness of the present book?

It has at least this usefulness: that the group of modern believers who are disappointed with the official Church teachings, a small herd perhaps, who are searching for liberating answers, can find in the thoughts expressed in this book such answers; and that the precious light of truth will no longer remain hidden under the bushel of uncritical opinions.

However, whether we see the resurrection of Jesus in modern or pre-modern terms, for our profession of faith we are in both cases equally dependent on witnesses. There are two sorts of these: a few short direct communications and a series of stories, which, depending on their date, become longer and more colourful. More about these stories soon. The direct communications will be dealt with first.

The Direct Communications

These are limited for the most part to vv.4-8 of chapter 15 of Paul's First Epistle to the Corinthians. This letter must have been written about 25 years after the death of Jesus. The oldest narrative text, on the other hand, the extremely brief chapter 16 of Mark's gospel, dates from 15 to 20 years later. There are no earlier witnesses apart from a casual remark in the First Epistle to the Christians in Thessaloniki (5:4) from the year 51. Precisely this casualness shows that belief in the resurrection of Jesus gave rise to no worries or questions, so that by that time it was already taken for granted.

For Paul, Jesus' resurrection follows logically from the experience that he had let himself be seen after his death. He was alive (again), no longer lay in the grave, and was therefore risen. This reasoning is correct, at least if one starts with the Jewish conception of man as a body animated by a soul. It is no longer correct, if one starts with the Greek conception of man, according to which the essence of man is the spiritual and therefore immortal soul, which in death is freed from its outer shell. For spiritual realities are fundamentally invisible. Jesus' condition after death would be comparable with that of a butterfly which is freed from its chrysalis and no longer needs to be concerned with it.

The "Seeing" which Paul evokes

Paul speaks, naturally, as a Jew, and in his Jewish way of thinking a risen person is a body animated by a soul and as such is visible and audible. When he then says that Jesus let himself be seen after his death, he seems to refer to the physiological process of seeing that we know. Precisely this physiological seeing would confirm the bodily resurrection of Jesus, which is a stumbling block for the modern believer. But sight can also be a purely psychological process, in which very intense inner experiences are unconsciously projected outwards, in such a way that they give the convincing impression of belonging to material reality out there. Paul names Peter as the first of these seers and after him the twelve (or should he have written the eleven?). These had more than any others experienced the aura of Jesus while he was still alive. It can therefore be supposed that they experienced his aura more intensively than the others, after he had attained his fullness of life in death. With those listed by Paul afterwards, it could be that the witness of Peter and the eleven activated their own "seeing". With regard to the puzzling text about the "more than 500 brethren (and sisters?) simultaneously" (15:6) who are supposed to have "seen" Jesus, it could have been a collective ecstatic experience of a large group; similar experiences are referred to in the Acts of the Apostles 2:4 and 7-11 (the Pentecost story) or 4:31 and 10:44-46 (both times echoing the Pentecost events).

The certainty that Jesus was alive and remained active was reinforced by experiences of renewal and well-being similar to those which Jesus' activity had previously brought about. Luke had no problem with relating cures, worked by the early Church, as being effected by the risen Jesus. We only need to compare the healing of the lame man in chapter 3 of the Acts of the Apostles with the healing of the lame man in chapter 5 of John's gospel. Both are equally impossible and therefore invented. Anyone who has been lame for 38 years, as in John's gospel, or from birth as in the Acts of the Apostles, has no leg muscles and no sense of balance. Still, the lame man in John's gospel can, at Jesus' word, stand up, take up his bed and walk away; and in the Acts of the Apostles he can, on Peter's command, jump up and go into the temple with Peter and John. Peter gives him that order in the name of Jesus of Nazareth, and "name" in the Bible is something different from a combination of letters for identification purposes. It is a Semitic paraphrase for the person and his aura. The story of this cure serves to confirm that the power radiated by the historical Jesus is now radiated by him through the community that believes in him. And that shows that he lives on in the community.

One final comment about "seeing". Paul relates three times in the Acts of the Apostles his seeing of Jesus in the story of his conversion on the way to Damascus. Three times he sees only a blinding light. Nowhere does he say that he sees the glorified Jesus, and yet he puts his own "seeing" on the same level as that of Peter and the twelve. When in Galatians 1:15-16 he then looks back at his conversion, he formulates it without mentioning the seeing (and hearing) which is mentioned every time in the Acts of the Apostles. He merely says: "When it pleased God to reveal his Son to me." Clearly it was a question of a revealing inner vision, the opening of his inner eye to a truth which he had sensed for a long time without wanting to acknowledge it.

The Apparition Stories and the "Holy Sepulchre"

Reports or stories about the resurrection itself are to be found only in a few apocryphal documents and are simply bizarre. The early Church rightly rejected them. The four canonical gospels have only stories about Jesus' appearances. In Mark's gospel these take up only 8 verses, to which a second hand later added another 12, derived from the other gospels. In Matthew these 8 verses have become 20, in Luke even 53 plus another 11 at the beginning of his Acts of the Apostles, and finally in John 66. Every year these stories are read at the Easter church services and have thereby decisively shaped what the faithful take the resurrection to mean. Only since the Enlightenment have people become aware that they are not accounts of real events but are intended to give readers a vital message about Jesus.

The stories begin, as a rule, at the same point: namely, the empty grave. This then serves as a reliable proof that Jesus has risen. Twenty years earlier that was by no means the case. Paul does not say one word about the empty grave. His preaching of the resurrection is completely based on the idea that the risen Jesus "had shown himself", this "showing" leading naturally to the certainty that Jesus must have awoken from his sleep of death and risen up and left his grave and that consequently the grave is empty. With Paul this logical conclusion is still unspoken. The empty grave is a later but obvious development.

15 years after Paul, Mark speaks quite differently about the resurrection of Jesus. Not the "sight" of the risen Jesus is any longer the basis of his belief in the resurrection, but the empty grave. In his story, a young man clad in white (the white garb indicates a heavenly being) sits in the chamber of the grave and explicitly links Jesus' being risen with the emptiness of the grave. "He has risen, says the youth, (for) he is not here (any more)." For lack of written witnesses we cannot know whether oral tradition as early as the time of Paul linked the resurrection of Jesus with the empty grave. In any case, the written tradition regarding this link begins with Mark. The other three evangelists clearly rely on him. With Paul, the fact that the grave had to be empty remains completely in the background as an unspoken

consequence. But in Mark's gospel the empty grave dominates the foreground and, instead of "seeing", becomes the decisive argument for the bodily resurrection of Jesus. Of course, an empty grave is not, of itself, proof that the buried person must have "risen". Other explanations are also possible. The Jewish authorities put forward one possibility (Matthew 27:64) and Magdalen a similar one (John 20:13). But for Mark the empty grave removes all doubt.

This interest in the empty grave results in an ever stronger emphasis on the physical character of the resurrection. For Mark the empty grave does prove that Jesus must have risen, although for the time being there is no trace of Him. For Matthew, Jesus already appears to the women who have come to the grave. They are even able to embrace his feet (28:9). For Luke the disciples are able to feel his flesh and bones (24:39) and Jesus enjoys eating a piece of fried fish (24:43-44), which points to his having normal digestive functions. For John, finally, Thomas can put his finger into the nail wound and his hand into the wound in Jesus' side.

Emphasis on the physical aspect of the risen Jesus naturally makes it impossible to understand his "resurrection" as a symbolical expression for the mysterious event that has taken place in Jesus as he dies. From here on, the physical moving out of the grave is seen as the proper account of this mysterious event and even as the essential aspect of it. The "going to the Father" or the "sitting at the right hand of the Father", visual biblical synonyms for the resurrection, are later reduced to having only incidental status which could be done without.

Such an emphasis on the physical aspect makes for modern people belief in the resurrection completely impossible. Mark is responsible for this, because he was the one who began to link the resurrection explicitly to an empty grave chamber. On the other hand precisely in this way he made the message of the resurrection accessible to a culture whose thinking was still mythological.

But speaking of "resurrection" presupposes the custom of burial. With cremation the concept loses its point of reference and its visual force. That explains why the Enlightenment consciously propagated cremation, as a means to demonstrate clearly the impossibility of the "resurrection of the flesh". And that explains, conversely, why Church authorities reacted so vigorously against cremation, which in itself is only a cultural custom, and forbade it, judging (according to the decree of 1924) that this "barbaric custom" undermined faith in the resurrection. The Church authorities thereby identified the image with the reality, whereas the image only points to the reality. They stared at the pointing finger instead of looking in the direction to which the finger pointed.

This materializing also had consequences for the "third day", which likewise has to be regarded as symbolical. It is already part of Paul's preaching about the resurrection. Paul even thinks that the bible predicted this third day. But there is nothing in the Bible about such a prediction. At the most, the third day is seen as the day of a crucial rescuing intervention by Yahweh. Yet this symbolically understood third day has soon become a chronological date. Thus Mark had the resurrection of Jesus, understood by him as physical, take place on the day after the Sabbath, and since then it has up to the present been taken for granted that the grave was empty on the Sunday morning. Anyone who would have dared to maintain that the corpse of Jesus lay even after the third day cold and stiff in the grave, perhaps even in a mass grave, and then slowly began to decay, would up to the 18th century have paid for this with his life, whether under Protestant or Catholic regimes. The conviction that the grave was empty, to which conviction for centuries painters and sculptors, showing Jesus rising in triumph from his tomb, have made their contribution, proves that a pre-modern culture needed precisely this quite clear notion in order to assimilate the message of the resurrection. To this extent Mark's notion has been a blessing for the initial "naivety", i.e. for pre-modern faith.

That explains also the veneration of Jesus's grave during the whole of Church history, although its exact localization in Jerusalem at first was unknown and had to be invented. According to Eusebius of Caesarea the biographer, or more accurately, the panegyrist, of the emperor Constantine the grave was accidentally found during the demolition of a Venus temple. It was not expected to be found there, which means that its whereabouts were not known. Every grave that was found, could count as Jesus' grave. The basilica built by Constantine over the supposed grave of Jesus became one of the most sacred monuments in Christianity and the "Holy Sepulchre" became the object of ever increasing veneration. The ill-fated crusades were aimed at liberating it from the Muslims. An Order of the Knights of the Holy Sepulchre was founded, and in the Tyrol and in Bavaria there are still many churches where in Holy Week a "Holy Sepulchre" is set up and venerated. This veneration is basically strange, since a grave is a symbol of death and extinction, not a symbol of life. Besides, the Holy Sepulchre is a stumbling block for modernity. For it presupposes that Jesus' corpse had become alive again and, of itself, had left the burial chamber. Here modernity says: no. And it cannot say otherwise. There are such things as the laws of nature.

Critical Analysis of Mark's Conception

But what does an exact analysis of the genuine Mark text (16:1-8) tell us about its historical worth? The text does begin, at any rate, in a seemingly historical tone. The concluding verses of chapter 15 had related Jesus' burial and the presence of the women at this burial, but bear in mind the critical comments about this burial in the previous chapter of this book. The initial verses of chapter 16 deal then with the visit of these woman to the grave on Sunday morning. Here questions immediately arise. Why do they want to anoint Jesus' corpse 36 hours after his death? And why in such an early hour? And even though they know that they are not capable of rolling the stone away from the tomb? These questions disappear of course automatically, if we accept that this whole narrative is unhistorical.

But this arrival of the women is closely connected with the discovery that the stone has been rolled away. By whom? Matthew saw the problem and gave his answer: by an angel. Mark, for his part, remains wisely silent about it. But angels who appear and roll a heavy stone away are only to be found in mythology, for they presuppose a second world which intervenes in ours. Precisely this seamless transition from history to mythology casts a dubious light on the historical character of what was supposedly an historical beginning

In Mark's gospel the angel is there also, in the form of a young man. And the grave is empty. If that is supposed to be historical fact (but we have to keep in mind the seamless transition in the story from history to myth!) how is it to be explained? In the context of the gospel, naturally, by saying that Jesus has come back to life and has left the grave. But for a modern believer something so obviously mythological is not acceptable. One must conclude that the empty grave in Mark's gospel is only a mythological and therefore unhistorical expression of his own faith that Jesus is "risen", i.e. that he is alive. The same must be said, then, of the three other evangelists, for they work busily at the further development of Mark's story.

For Mark, Jesus does not as yet appear. Only an angel appears. And although he tells the women to report Jesus' resurrection to the disciples, they don't do it. But then how could the news about the resurrection reach the disciples? Besides, where were they? As has been said above, after Jesus was captured, they would not have looked for somewhere to stay in Jerusalem, nor would Peter, after his denial, have stayed there any longer.

Matthew reinforces the mythological element in Mark's story. He adds an earthquake and a blindingly white angel, who in a moment rolls away a ton-weight stone and causes the guards to panic so much that they fall down as if dead. A new element in Matthew is that Jesus now appears to the women. The whole story of the guards and the rumour which they spread in the city at the behest of the chief priests is invented, just as much as is the empty grave itself. Probably what is reflected here is an apologetic discussion which Matthew had in Jewish circles. In Matthew's gospel, the tensions between Christians and Jews often become apparent.

Luke's text remains closer to that of Mark. In Luke, too, the stone is already rolled away, but now two men appear from another world, and this time the women do bring the message of Jesus' resurrection to the disciples. But the disciples do not believe them. As for John, he takes over some things from the three synoptics, like the role of Mary Magdalen, Peter's running to the grave, the comment about the linen. Everything else is new. Even the touching scene of Jesus' meeting with Mary Magdalen (19:2-10). This is clearly a later insertion into his narration; above it has been suggested that this fourth gospel may have gone through several hands. That it is a later insertion is clear from an analysis of the time sequences. Mary, who according to verse 1 is supposed to have run to the disciples, is in verse 11 still weeping at the grave, which means that she has not run to the disciples. Besides, they were probably no longer in

Jerusalem. And if they were nevertheless there, hiding somewhere for fear of the Jewish authorities (20:19), how could Peter and the mysterious disciple have dared to run to the grave, traversing the city in the broad light of day? And how did they know where it was? Since this race plays absolutely no further role in the narrative and could therefore just as easily have been omitted, this scene is best interpreted symbolically, as a comment inserted here (but why here?) by the evangelist about the relationship between the official Church (Peter) and the charismatic (the mysterious disciple), which even as early as those days was not altogether an easy one.

Anyone who, despite of all the conclusive arguments of modernity, remains caught up with the pre-modern, mythological notion of the resurrection event, must after this analysis admit that such an amount of contradictions disqualifies the historical value of the story. Not only the number of apparitions but also the time and place and the persons vary without embarrassment. It is also noticeable that from one evangelist to the next the stories become longer, more varied, and more colourful. Only the storyteller's imagination can take the liberty of presenting the same theme in different ways.

But if the empty grave in Mark's gospel and in the later evangelists is of a mythological nature, what is its hidden meaning? Myths are always images of deeper realities. The empty grave can be seen as a photographic negative, the positive image of which is the traditionally understood "resurrection". In the Bible and then in Mark the "grave" is mostly a symbolic concept for death. To be buried means to go down into the underworld, the realm of the dead. That the grave is found empty on the third day means that the underworld has not been able to keep its grip on Jesus, that he has shown himself stronger than death. Despite his death he is alive (again). For Mark this positive statement is the essence of his message.

But this message is not to be understood biologically. We speak also quite "un-biologically" of the living God. But Mark most probably understood the resurrection of Jesus as biological. The other three evangelists, who used him as their source, certainly did. This can be seen clearly from the details of their apparition stories which become steadily more material. But they all lived in an intellectual climate steeped in mythology, where for God everything is possible. Above, it has been said that in modernity it is better not to use the word resurrection any longer, but, instead, other expressions like fulfilment, glorification, eternal life, ultimate union with the love which is God. That fulfilment or union was for Jesus not the automatic result of his barbarous execution. It is not this which fulfilled Him, but his decision to bring to his people, even at the cost of his life, the message that God is love. It was his love of his fellow men that brought about his fulfilment, so that he now lives in fullness. Not through the cruelty of his enemies, and therefore not through death as such did he become one with the Fundamental Love, for otherwise his executioners would be our saviours, but only through his selflessness. It is therefore wrong, at a funeral, to use the image of the grain of wheat going into the ground, to proclaim, as a consolation, that the deceased in dying has entered eternal life with God. We do enter this life only according to the measure of love for our fellow men that we have achieved. Otherwise every murderer would have done his victim a priceless service.

If the empty grave is mythology, then, of course, so are the stories of the apparitions. The very fact that in these stories Jesus appears and disappears at will, shows that he is no longer bothered by the laws of our cosmos. But then he neither belongs to our cosmos any longer, and what he says or does in these apparitions does not have the slightest historical reality. That does not mean that these stories cannot have a quite moving effect on the believer, as, for example, the encounter of Mary Magdalen with the risen Jesus, whom she takes to be the gardener, or the story of the two Emmaus disciples, or the miraculous catch of fish. But they remain freely invented short stories, creations of an inspired author, and not reports.

This has important consequences. Church authorities can, for example, no longer refer to John 20:23 to consider themselves as having the power to forgive or not to forgive sins. Besides, as already mentioned above, here lurks a conception of sin which makes of God a judge and makes of forgiveness a remission of debt without existential renewal on the part of the sinner. Neither did Jesus give the mandate in Matthew 28:19 to baptize all peoples in the name (whatever this may mean) of the Father and of the Son and of the Holy Spirit, any more than, at the Lake of Gennesaret, he appointed Peter as shepherd of the flock, the Church. For anyone who has gone through the gate of death is no longer a player on the field of history, not even Jesus. We can only have recourse to what he said and did before his death. The Jesus who has reached his fulfilment, is completely beyond our grasp and the stories about his appearing have no historical value. This means, of course, that the foundations on which many a theological edifice is erected collapse in a terrifying way.

Do these stories therefore teach us nothing? Of course they teach us something. They teach us that within a few decades the message that Jesus, despite his death on the cross, still lives creatively, has not only taken root, but even such strong roots that new impulses continually spring from them. They teach us also how the early Church saw Jesus, for the stories of the apparitions depict him naturally as he was known before his death or as he had been portrayed by the preachers. To this extent they can be regarded as witnesses of his historical activity.

The True Foundation of our Belief in the Resurrection

But can Paul's statement in the First Epistle to the Corinthians that he and a few other people “saw” Jesus after his death, be a solid foundation for believing that Jesus is alive? The German exegete Gerd Lüdemann points out, in an extremely critical study of the apparition stories, that almost the whole weight of our belief in the resurrection of Jesus rests on the “seeing” of Peter. In 1 Corinthians 15 he is introduced by Paul as the first and, in this sense, the most crucial witness. An echo of this is found in Luke 24:34, when the disciples greet the two who have returned from Emmaus, with the jubilant cry: “He has risen and appeared to Simon!” Lüdemann explains Peter's “seeing” psychologically – a result of the devastating blow that his denial of Jesus had meant for him. His self-image was completely destroyed and in his shattered psyche a burning desire to make good his mistake awakened in him after some time the illusion of seeing Jesus alive again in front of him. Through a kind of chain reaction his own hallucination would have produced a similar experience in the other disciples.

If this were to be the case, Christianity, with all that it has changed for the good in human history, would have been ultimately the product of an illusion. This conclusion is of itself already enough to refute Lüdemann's thesis, for illusions do not produce reality and do not improve the world. Instead, after a time they are unmasked by reality and disposed of. In the long run people's eyes are opened. Even when a charismatic guru or leader succeeds for a long time in fascinating followers, his movement has, as a rule, already faded long before his death. Let us suppose for a moment that Peter was such a charismatic person, who, driven by his hallucination, was able to convince his listeners that Jesus was alive again. But how can we explain that these listeners, who had themselves seen nothing, were able to create the same illusion in their own listeners, and then these again in *their* listeners, and so on until today, 2000 years later?

On what, then, is our own belief in the resurrection based? On our own "seeing" of the living Jesus. This "seeing" is the fruit of preaching. The story of the two Emmaus disciples can be read as a parable of this process. The stranger who leads the two to the joyous awareness that Jesus lives, is the preacher of faith. He makes his own inner vision light up in the two, his own experience of meaning and fulfilment which he shares in by turning to Jesus as to a living person. No spark springs from cold ashes, life does not emerge from a dead person. No reasoning can cope with this experience of life and fulfilment. This applies to the reasoning of Lüdemann as well.

If we accept that the Church (understood as the whole community of those who believe in Jesus) is born of the encounter of these believers with the living Jesus and has made this figure of Jesus visible in many guises down through the centuries, then it is no presumption to say that it will interpret his figure better than someone who does not believe in him. What we mean by the "resurrection of Jesus" is therefore crucial to the answer to the question posed in the title of this book: Jesus of Nazareth, a Person Like us? Obviously, the answer must be: yes and no. This is to be explained in more detail in the final chapter.

CHAPTER SEVEN

Concluding Observations

What is, for the time being, the last of the series of books which we could call attempts at a biography of Jesus, is the book by Reza Aslan, *The Zealot,* mentioned above, which has already stirred up some dust. Because *The Zealot* was the inducement to write the present book, it is to be looked at here, in conclusion, more in detail. Like innumerable authors before him, Aslan wanted to bring to light who this Jesus of Nazareth really was, who both attracted him powerfully and at the same time was for him a source of many questions. The many mythological and unhistorical elements in the gospels and the contradictory conclusions drawn from them in scientific Bible criticism had in Aslan's opinion made the real Jesus disappear in a fog. With the aid of reliable historical data about the social and political climate in which the life of Jesus was played out, he wanted as far as possible to draw him out of the fog. For this climate could not have been without influence on the thinking and activity of Jesus. These data provide a means, according to Aslan, of bringing to light the often hidden meaning and intention of his words and activity. Using as a basis above all (and rightly) Flavius Josephus, the Jewish historian favoured by the Roman imperial dynasty of the Flavii, Aslan proceeds to present this climate to us. He is not the first to try in this way to find the historical Jesus. Alas, this starting point leads as a rule into a cul-de-sac. All that is left of Jesus at the end is a typically Jewish political Messiah. But where, then, does the enormous influence come from, which, 2000 years later, he still exerts world-wide?

In Aslan's account, Palestine at the time of Jesus was a seething kettle of unrest, violence, and blood-spilling, with the fires stoked by the exalted expectation that Yahweh would soon intervene and send His Messiah to liberate His oppressed people from Roman rule and make it powerful and prosperous again as in the (idealized!) times of King David. The Jewish Bible was full of this call for liberation, which traditionally had an explicitly social and political sound to it. In Jesus' lifetime this was more clearly the case than previously, as an expression of helpless protest against the greedy and brutal, even often cruel actions of the Roman occupying force, which also, in the eyes of the orthodox Jews, sullied with its cult of idols the land that belonged to Yahweh and which He had given for ever to His chosen people Israel. Yahweh could certainly no longer tolerate the heathens illegally occupying and exploiting His country. In this climate, which was pregnant with explosions, now and then charismatic leaders appeared who gave political shape to the unrealistic expectations and dreams of their people and dragged their followers into a futile rebellion against Rome. We can compare these all-too-willing rebels with the so-called fighters for God of the Islamic State, who hope through a suicide attack or through death in battle for the cause of Allah to get into paradise as martyrs. For the Jews the paradise they saw was a paradisiacal future for their suppressed people.

Critique of Aslan's Socio-Political Image of Jesus

This is the framework in which Aslan depicts Jesus. For him Jesus is one of the many tragically failed claimants to be the Messiah, but an admirable one, deeply religiously-inspired, a noble, human, generous fighter for the Kingdom of Yahweh. Aslan's picture seems plausible. And the pieces of the puzzle from which he puts his image of Jesus together are not of his own invention. He takes them from the gospel. Often we have to admit he is right in his interpretation of the words and actions of Jesus. But more often we have to introduce some serious question marks. To separate the chaff from the wheat, a detailed discussion of his book would be needed, but there is not space for that here. A general criticism would be that he works very selectively, uses what fits his view, omits what contradicts it and presents possibilities as facts. But he does it with so much verve and stylistic skill that the reader who is less familiar with the gospels is in danger of uncritically accepting his view as the right one. Precisely this is what makes an answer which shows things in their correct light highly desirable.

For his picture of Jesus Aslan refers above all to Jesus' entry into Jerusalem on Palm Sunday and to the main theme of Jesus' preaching: the coming of the Kingdom of God. As Mark 11:1-11 makes clear, Jesus himself consciously set up the scene of his entry into Jerusalem: he has two of his disciples find an ass. The details of this search present him as a clairvoyant, although he was not one. That is what tradition made of him after his death, since it was more concerned with glorifying him than with historical truth. As he enters the city, he lets himself be honoured as the "Son of David", a biblical equivalent of "Messiah" and therefore of "King of Israel", for the term "Messiah" taken from the Hebrew means "The Anointed", and in Israel, where kings were anointed, not crowned, this meant "King". Aslan thinks that to let himself be honoured as Messiah amounted to a declaration of war against Rome and was the direct cause of his execution as a rebel. But then why Rome would wait five days to react remains unexplained. And the capture of Jesus was not carried out by the Romans, but by the Jewish temple guards. Aslan maintains without the slightest proof that kings occasionally rode ceremoniously into their city on an ass. Such unfounded statements are, of course, worthless.

The second element on which Aslan bases his argument in presenting Jesus as a political prophet is his interpretation of the main theme of Jesus' preaching, the coming of God's reign, for the reign of God is exactly what is meant by the Kingdom of God. For Aslan, this reign consists in Yahweh ruling as sole king over His own land, which the Romans have illegally taken over. But before that could become reality, the Roman usurpers must of course be chased out of His land, and that could not happen without force and bloodshed. Jesus knew that and, according to Aslan, was also ready for this fight. Also Jesus' answer to the question about the emperor's tax (Mark 12:17), that one should render to God the things that are God's, is interpreted by Aslan (very freely!) in this sense: the land of Israel, which belongs to Yahweh and which the Roman Emperor has stolen from Him, must be given back to Him.

Definitely there were amongst Jesus' followers some who cherished political expectations. We can see this from, amongst other things, the attempt of the sons of Zebedee, James and John, to secure for themselves the most important functions in the coming Kingdom of God, as they imagined it, and from the ensuing reaction of the other ten to this ugly manoeuvre (Mark 10:35-41), which threatened their own chances of advancement. And why did some of Jesus' disciples, at least two of them, carry swords (Luke 22:38) and were ready to strike, as Jesus was being captured (Luke 22:49)? If we had only these and similar elements to go by, we could perhaps admit that Aslan is right and think that the 2000 years of Christian belief amounted to one enormous error.

But if we do not read the gospels selectively, as he did, a quite different image of Jesus emerges. Aslan's political interpretation of the Kingdom of God, which makes of Jesus a fighter for God prepared to use violence, contradicts many other words of his about the Kingdom of God which clearly advocate the contrary, such as the parable of the mustard seed or the silently growing seed (Mark 4:26-32), or his words that we have to be like children, if we are to enter the Kingdom of God (Mark 10:14 or Matthew 11:2-5), or when in his Sermon on the Mount he calls the humble and the peace-makers blessed (Matthew 5:5-9), or when he formulates the Golden Rule in these positive terms: "Do unto others as you would wish them to do to you" (Matthew 7:12), or when he gives the warning not to retaliate (Matthew 6:39-41) but rather to overcome evil with good (as Paul will formulate it in his Epistle to the Romans, 12:21), or when he calls on them to be servants rather than masters (Mark 10:42-44). It is precisely with these last words that he puts paid to the political ambitions of the brothers James and John.

Against this background, his entry into Jerusalem appears in a quite different light. It becomes a message without words about how the Messiah sent by Yahweh is to appear on his arrival: not as a victorious ruler, but as a gentle and peace-loving fellow human being, who in this way shows what Yahweh Himself is like. And the cleansing of the temple, which Aslan is not wrong in interpreting as a direct attack on the Jewish establishment, and thereby indirectly (with doubtful justification) as an attack on Roman rule to which this establishment owed its position of authority, can be interpreted differently. Jesus' words in his outburst of indignation are not an expression of any socio-political vision but rather of a mystical and prophetical inspiration of the moment.

Undoubtedly there lived in a part of the Jewish population something of the mentality of today's political fighters for God's cause. But according to what the gospels show us of Jesus, this was not the vision on which his life was based. We cannot conclude from the social and political circumstances and events of his time that Jesus thought and felt likewise, no more than we can deduce the mentality of a Socrates from the political ideas and modes of behaviour of the Athenian citizens in the 5th

century BC. We only have to think of their Machiavellian power politics in their treatment of the inhabitants of the island of Melos. That was not Socrates' way of thinking and acting – quite the contrary.

The Resurrection of Jesus as the Decisive Answer

But the ultimate justification for rejecting not only Aslan's Jesus image, but all non-Christian Jesus images, is expressed by Aslan himself, without his drawing conclusions from it, namely the inexplicable historical fact that more and more people, despite resistance and persecution, have found it meaningful to believe with their whole heart in this failed Messiah. This shows that they have found in him not a miraculous healer or a political reformer, but someone in whose life and words they sensed to an intense degree the presence of God. That is why they had confidence in his message and chose his thinking and acting as a norm for their own thinking and acting. That explains that he is the only historical figure to have become after his death the object of a religious veneration which has not been a flash in the pan. This veneration has become ever deeper and, in the course of the centuries, has even become deification. Aslan himself admits: "The most obvious reason for taking the resurrection experiences of the disciples seriously, is that Jesus is the only one of the many Messiahs who preceded and followed him to be still called the Messiah."

But taking these experiences seriously surely means admitting, as contradictory as it might seem, that the Jesus who was executed under Pontius Pilate is alive; still more, that he radiates life, attracts people, binds them to himself and moves them to ever greater human development. In the previous chapter the attempt was made to clarify for people in the modern age the meaning of this seemingly contradictory message about a dead man who is alive. That Jesus "lives" is, namely, not biological language but the language of faith based on experience, a language that tries to express that Jesus has become of one essence with the Ultimate Ground of all life, a union through which he shares in God's eternity.

The Redemption and the Resurrection of the Dead Translated into Modern Concepts

When Jesus dreamed of a new Israel as the beginning of a renewed humanity (he had read in the prophets the prediction about this renewal), his inspiration was not the narrow political dream attributed to him by Aslan, but rather the vision of the prophet Isaiah that in Israel the wolf and the lamb would one day live in peace with one another, and that from Israel the glory of God would be radiated out into the entire world. For Jesus it was clear that the true liberation of man consists in his growing humanization and that this is not the product of power, but the fruit of selfless service. He put this intuition into practice himself, and the more people follow him along this path, the more he gradually realizes the new creation of the world. The language in which the community of believers expressed their faith in him in pre-modern times, was that he has redeemed us, has bought us free, has saved us, has made us just, has reconciled us with God by his blood. Today we would say instead: being filled himself with the Fundamental Love, which is God, and moved by it, he moves us by his power of attraction to be like him, he inspires us, he fills us with attitudes like his, he makes new people of us and in this way gradually brings about a restored world.

According to the extent that we allow ourselves to be influenced by Him, we all share in his “resurrection”, i.e. in his unity with the Fundamental Love, and rise up with him to ultimate life. Already now. We confess this more or less consciously where it concerns those whom we revere as saints. To honour them means indeed to see them as living and inspiring us, and therefore as “risen”. This “resurrection” is the fruit of their union with the living Jesus, which has grown in them by their having let themselves be penetrated with his attitude and frame of mind. Unconsciously we were always aware that despite their death they are living, for we have never honoured and implored the *souls* of the saints, not even on pilgrimages to their burial place or to their mummified remains under an altar. No, we have always honoured themselves. And when saints appear (it is said of Mary that she does that often), those who see them, have never doubted that they saw the saints themselves, rather than their soul. They honestly thought that a supernatural world to which in their eyes the dead now belong, had broken into our world order. But in thinking this they were heirs to a pre-modern worldview. And we are not that any more. What the psychological process was that brought about their impression that they saw an apparition can be passed over here.

But what is true of the saints, is true of every person, according to the extent to which he has let himself be led by love. And everyone does that to some extent. The Fundamental Love, which is God, produces every person as a partial expression of Himself and impels him then naturally in the direction of love. The saints distinguish themselves from average people only by listening to this impulse in a no longer merely average way. Not their penitential exercises or their "holy anorexia" or their long prayers or their mystical experiences have made them holy, but only their selflessness. But since every person, if only a tiny bit now and then, lets himself be moved by love, everyone survives death, if only a tiny bit.

To let oneself be moved by love it is not absolutely necessary to know Jesus or his message. Although to know him and the attraction that springs from this knowledge is a powerful help to let ourselves be led by love, we nevertheless encounter marvels of humanity totally apart from a Christian context. It can be said of such people, who live like this on the basis of Love-God's impulse, that just as the saints in death they "resurrect". The creative influence in the course of the centuries of a Socrates, a Gautama Buddha, a Lao-Tzu, a Mahatma Gandhi makes their "resurrection" even visible. Life radiates around, is creative. But because they have lived outside the Jewish-Christian tradition, the term "resurrection" not used in relation to them. This term is reserved in our culture for Jesus of Nazareth. Wrongly so. There is no basis for reserving "resurrection", and the eternal life linked to it, for Jesus and his followers.

This brings us to a modern and meaningful way of interpreting the last article of the Credo: the resurrection of the dead or, as it was called in those days, of the flesh. This article of faith sounds almost comical to modern ears. The billions of people reduced to dust (or even less) in the course of history are suddenly to rise again, alive and well, with flesh and bones, awakened out of the sleep of death by the trumpets of the Last Judgement? This was the pre-modern view. The terrifying "Dies Irae" paints that in words, the famous frescos of Luca Signorelli in the Capella Nuova of the cathedral in Orvieto paint it in colours. But if, as above, we understand "resurrection" to mean man's going victoriously through death in the measure that he has loved, this incomprehensibility and the annoyance connected with it disappears. Then each one "resurrects" to the greater or lesser degree to which the divine seed in the depths of his being has had the possibility of developing. And each one "resurrects" not at the Last Judgement but at his own death. Like Jesus himself.

This throws a new light on the intimate connection between the resurrection of Jesus and that of the faithful, which Paul highlights so passionately in his letter to the Corinthians: "If he has not risen, there is no resurrection for us, and if there is no resurrection for us, neither has he risen from the dead" (1 Corinthians 15:12 and 16). And it also becomes clear why in the same context he calls Jesus the firstborn of many brothers (and sisters, of course): the same union with the Holy Mystery, God, as the fruit of love, is present in Jesus in superabundance and in the brothers and sisters according to the measure of their human limitations.

Jesus of Nazareth, a Person Like Us?

The book began with this question. It can also now be answered, and, indeed, as could be expected and has already been said above: with yes and no. With this yes is meant that he is no citizen of another world, no alien who for a short time pitched his tent with us, not an all-knowing, almighty miracle worker and magician, not the "only begotten" Son of God, who has come down to us from heaven in human form with a two-fold consciousness: a divine and a human, whereas we have to be satisfied with a limited human consciousness, but a person like us, with the same needs, desires and reactions that we have. In the gospels we see him fast, but also feast, even giving his enemies a welcome chance to call him a glutton and a drunk; we see Him, weary from walking, sitting at the edge of a well or lying asleep in a boat in stormy weather, standing at a fig tree hungrily looking for figs and being angry that it does not bear any, not hiding his disappointment about how little success he has in finding a willing ear for his message. For a time he was even dependent on the charismatic personality of John the Baptist. All very human. And he felt the same horror that anyone feels at being dragged off to be tortured; and he felt in his flesh the same dreadful pain of anyone who is being scourged and nailed to a cross. As a person like us he must have had the same sexual needs as we have, but clearly he managed them differently from the way average people manage them. He was not dependent on these needs, but was inwardly free, with the same freedom which he revealed with regard to money, position and his opponents' criticism.

That he was a person like us means also that he was to a great extent determined by the cultural ideas and conceptions of his time, as we are by ours. That is the origin of his expectation that the Kingdom of Yahweh and the defeat of evil in the world would soon come about – in which he was later seen to be wrong. It is also the origin of his division of reality into two worlds, as in the Torah: the world of Yahweh and our world, in which Yahweh can intervene whenever He wishes. Or of his idea that he had to concern himself only with Israel, an erroneous idea from which he was freed by his encounter with the Canaanite woman in Mark 7:24. Or of his taking for granted that illnesses were the work of devils from outside our world. Or of his geocentric view of the world with Heaven above and the world of the dead below. All that was conditioned by his time and did not represent truth merely because he thought that way.

That is the way we see Him. But how did he see himself? The question about his self-consciousness was already posed in chapter 4 and basically left unanswered. It is unanswerable indeed. What we can take from his own words in this regard is confusing and contradictory. The hundreds of critical studies since the Enlightenment have led precisely to this insight. What exactly he said and also what he meant by it remains veiled in fog. The idea that we could attribute this contradictoriness to Jesus himself does not match with the wisdom and clarity which speaks out of his other words. Therefore it must originate from the community of his followers. The many words attributed to Jesus in John's gospel have to be completely disregarded here. They are not his, no more than his words in the apparition stories are his. These words have no historical validity.

But we can say this one thing with unquestionable certainty: he never saw himself as the only begotten Son of God, as God in human form. He was also not seen as such by his disciples. The Church started this only much later. The title "son of God" had, for Him, no other meaning than the one it had in the purely monotheistic Old Testament.

Did he see himself as the Messiah? Not as the political Messiah as Aslan would have it. It is noticeable that, according to Mark 8:27 and Matthew 1:11, the people did not see him as the Messiah. Only Peter, as spokesman of the Twelve, does, but he forbids them to speak about it. Why? Perhaps to guard against false expectations? But, along with "Lord", the title of "Messiah" is the most frequent one used for him by the early Church after his death. In the Pauline epistles it occurs with great frequency. It became merged with his real name to become: Jesus Christ.

How did he see the Kingdom of God, about which he frequently spoke, which was near, and the coming of which he watched out for? It did not mean in his view a social and political liberation, it was something existential, something in the human heart. It belonged, in any case, to God's future. But despite this future aspect he could say in Luke 11:20 that his exorcisms showed it had already begun, and in Luke 17:21 he says – even to the Pharisees! – that it was already "in them", or, with another translation of the preposition: was already "amongst them".

Also what he says about the Son of Man is confusing. He often uses this expression, and he is also the only one who uses it. This is where the contradictions are at their worst. Did he understand himself to be the heavenly Son of Man mentioned in Daniel 7:13-14? Mostly he distinguishes himself from this figure coming in the clouds who will once and for all transform human history, but sometimes he seems to identify himself with this Son of Man, which then implies his death and his coming again in this mythical form and also his resurrection. Or did he see himself rather as the suffering Servant of God from Isaiah 53, and did he think that he was soon to be executed, and that this was even part of his mission? If not, why did he remain on the Mount of Olives and wait to be captured? This knot cannot be unravelled.

Where does this confusion come from? Perhaps the early Church put some of these statements into Jesus' mouth as an expression of their faith in him, mixed with authentic words of Jesus which had become isolated from their original context, and Mark then loyally handed them on without thinking of the contradictions which this process had to bring with it. "Mark's account", writes Albert Schweitzer in his *Geschichte der Leben-Jesu-Forschung* (p.385), "is full of unclear things and contradictions", and he follows this with two full pages of examples of such unresolved issues.

The person of Jesus of Nazareth thus remains veiled in mists. In spiritual literature, friendship with Jesus is often spoken of. But these mists already make such language dubious. Besides, friendship requires reciprocity. Friends should meet on the same level. But Jesus reached his essential perfection and no longer belongs to the level of imperfection to which we belong. We cannot, therefore, enjoy friendship with Him, no more than we can with another dead person. We can remember Him, as in the Eucharist, admire, honour, love Him, and he can inspire us, attract us, move us to follow Him. That, and not friendship, is the right name for the relationship of the believer to the glorified Jesus of Nazareth.

Yet not *only* a person like us

The human qualities sketched above do not explain what it was that radiated out from him and what the synoptics' image of the transfiguration on the mountain represented. He was not just a person like us. That he walked across the lake at night and that he calmed the storm with a single word are further images used by the evangelists to express the mysterious element they sensed in Him. The disciples' question in the boat after he calmed the storm: "Who is he, that even the wind and the water obey Him?", is an indirect confession that they became aware of the presence of God in Him. His words and actions testify to an intimacy with the Fundamental Mystery, an intimacy which goes so far beyond the average human level that it is unattainable by us. Those who were affected by and caught up with this intimacy with God, have used all the means at their disposal to express their veneration. These were, as has already been said, Old Testament images and language forms – particularly the title: beloved son of God. This beloved son soon became the only son and, after 250 years, at the Council of Nicaea "the only begotten Son of God, born of the Father before all ages, true God from true God". The council arrived at this formulation by treating the language of lineage as real, whereas it was only the language of veneration in images through which the experience of Jesus' human transcendence had been expressed in the form of prayers already two hundred years previously. Jesus' human transcendence consisted essentially in his total selflessness, which is nothing but an intimate union with the selflessness of God. This human transcendence was then given a new interpretation, in which it was seen as a supernatural and absolute transcendence with overtones of omnipotence and sovereignty.

In the Christian tradition since Nicaea, Jesus as God from God naturally surpasses endlessly all other outstanding and, in this sense, transcending people: inspired sages and prophets and mystics like Moses, Gautama Buddha, Lao-Tzu, Mohammed, Mahatma Gandhi and so many other well-known and less well-known extraordinary people. But when he has come down from this heavenly throne and appears as a person like us, does it mean that these others can be seen simply as his equals, as often happens these days? What is then left of the uniqueness which used to be confessed with such conviction by his faithful? And what is left of the exclusiveness of the Christian faith as the way to human salvation? Is Jesus of Nazareth perhaps only one of many and not, as in the marvellous hymn in the Epistle to the Colossians 1:15-20, “the Firstborn of all creation, through whom and for whom everything was made, who exists before all things and in whom all things exist”, or is Peter wrong when he says in the Acts of the Apostles 4:12 to the Jewish authorities: “There is no other name under heaven through which we are to be saved”?

The exclusivity of Christianity as the way to salvation has already been relativized by Vatican II, where the conviction of today’s Church was formulated: that all confessions, each one in its own way, are paths to salvation, if not all in the same measure. But Vatican II remains true to the traditional certainty of faith, that Jesus is, like no other, the way to salvation, so that choosing this way has all the advantages. Naturally, there is nothing to prove this conviction. But arguments can be made for it. For example, we can point to the humanizing force of faith in Jesus the Messiah, that reveals itself amongst other things in the Christian commitment to the weak and those deprived of their human rights in society, and compare this with that which derives from other forms of faith. Or we can highlight the harmonious combination of inspiration and rationality in this faith, which is missing in many of the other religious confessions. We can also compare the persons mentioned above with Jesus, so far as we have reliable information about their lives, to show that none of them can compare with Jesus. But this leaves very broad scope for subjectivity.

But for a Christian these considerations are more than enough to allow him to choose confidently Jesus and his way. That means concretely to belong to his Church. "Church" (Scottish: Kirk) originates namely from the Greek adjective *kyriakè*, that itself is derived from the noun *kyrios*, Lord, and means therefore: related to the Lord (Jesus). This adjective qualified originally the later omitted noun *ekklèsia*, which meant: the official and democratic gathering of the people. Thus the *kyriakè (ekklèsia)* or community of the Lord (Jesus) did not at all designate an organization or an institution, but rather the community that adheres to Jesus of Nazareth and wants to follow his path.

The experience of human enrichment and fulfilment which the Christian enjoys in following this path is enough for him to dispel all doubt that this is the right way. He experiences in fact that in this he has chosen the better part and no longer needs to look for another way or to wait for the coming of another saviour. In John's gospel (6:68) Jesus asks his disciples whether they want to remain with him or not. Peter answers in the name of the others, and also in the name of all believing Christians: "To whom else should we go? Your words are the words of eternal life."